Getting Along

The Church's Quest for Unity
in a Polarized World

Endorsements

"In today's polarized society, in which no one seems to be able to find common ground with anyone else, Steve Pecota brings together biblical wisdom and insight from brilliant contemporary thinkers to create an important model for conversation that offers promise not only for rescuing unity in the Christian community, but also in society. Timely work indeed!"

—Joseph Castleberry, Ed.D.
President, Northwest University

"Steve Pecota's research highlights the importance of unity in the church by providing new insights into cultural and cognitive challenges to that unity. His skillful use of metaphorical language sparks numerous 'aha' moments, bringing useful insight applicable to one's particular questions, judgments, and circumstances. I strongly recommend this book for those seeking not only to diversify their church but diversify their relationships."

— Dr. James D. Croone, Sr.
Pastor of Risen Church Seattle WA
Author of *Seymour &Parham: The Move of God Amid Relationship and Conflict*

"When a work includes a contribution from the Greek Septuagint, and also a worthy observation from soccer coach, Ted Lasso, I have got to respect its eclectic sourcing! Steve Pecota ends up stressing our need for essential unity, not only identifying with new language our problems in getting there but also spelling out practical ways to move in that direction. Reading this will make you want to step out and try his suggestions!"

—Dr. C. David Gable
Director of Church Planting, SoCal Network (ret.)

"In a world where we often find ourselves asking with outrage, 'How could they actually believe that?!' Steve's question of us is calmer but no less of a challenge: Can the church pursue unity amid polarization? The journey to an answer is as compelling as the conclusion itself—you'll often find yourself saying, 'That's a great point; I hadn't thought of that!' as he explains how individuals arrive at judgments and decisions that are deeply divisive, and how he shows that practical attitudes and actions—not blanket agreement—build unity. With nuance, clarity, and insight, Steve presents a vision for pursuing unity in the church that restores my hope for reconciliation."

—Rebecca Rhoades, C.P.A., M.B.A.
Professor Emeritus, Evangel University

"I am happy to endorse Dr. Steve Pecota's new book, *Getting Along: The Church's Quest for Unity in a Polarized World*. I have the unique perspective of having watched Steve walk out his personal quest for church unity firsthand, as we were neighboring pastors and in a small group together for over twelve years. This book is not only a scholarly plea for unity in Christ's Church, but it is part of Steve's own heartbeat. This book is about learning and listening to one another in order to fulfill Jesus's prayer of John 17, 'that we may be one,' and while that level of unity may seem impossible now, it *will* happen. I am grateful for Dr. Pecota's work that will help move the church in this direction. May we become one in Christ!"

—Dr. Don Ross
Network Leader, Northwest Ministry Network

"I was thrilled to take in hand and read Stephen Pecota's timely book addressing the need for genuine unity in the body of Christ today in a culture riveted by discord and hostility toward anyone who may have a differing worldview. As a former colleague and friend who worked with Steve for nearly twenty years in Germany, I know that his desire to practically apply the teachings of Jesus in John 17 expresses his life's journey in ministry and is to be greatly commended. I like so much in the book; what stands out for this short recommendation, however, is that this work is not an ivory tower type of study but is very practical and down to earth even when the issues addressed are gritty and sometimes very unpleasant. We need to face the reality that our society is caught up sadly displaying toxic relational differences on moral and political issues—maybe as never before. Yet Steve's thorough work shows that there is still light at the end of the tunnel. Change is possible!"

—Dr. Paul Clark
Church Planter in German-Speaking Europe

"Dr. Stephen Pecota speaks to our divided cultural realities in a post-Covid world with incisiveness and care. Is Christian unity even possible considering the social rifts and politicized passions that have seeped into the church? Read *Getting Along* with a hopeful heart. As you do, pay careful attention to the strategic pathway that can lie before us. I have long respected Dr. Pecota and whole-heartedly commend this important book to you."

—James Bradford, PhD
Lead Pastor, Central Assembly of God, Springfield, Missouri

"I had the privilege of being part of Steve's research cohort for this book. Having worked with him directly and indirectly for years, I have seen the development of this material in his life—long before it became a research project. Steve has a unique background that undergirds his research. By connecting the work of Kahneman and Tversky, Galef and Haidt (among others) to the Church's quest for unity, Steve helps us understand this topic in a new way. In general, what does it take for us to see each other differently—and how do we know if we need to? This book will not only give you insight for your situation but also materials for training others."

—Dr. Kim Martinez
Groups Pastor, Shoreline Community Church

Getting Along

The Church's Quest for Unity
in a Polarized World

Stephen Pecota

Getting Along:
The Church's Quest for Unity in a Polarized World

Getting Along: The Church's Quest for Unity in a Polarized World by Stephen Pecota.

Edited by Lois E. Olena and Erica Huinda

ISBN: 979-8-9883372-0-1 Paperback
ISBN: 979-8-9883372-1-8 eBook

Dedication

To my wife, Karen—
my most important sounding board,
my most enduring encourager,
and my most delightful companion on our God-
directed journey.

Contents

Foreword

I first crossed paths with Steve over fifty years ago at Northwest University (NU), then a small Assemblies of God (AG) college near Seattle, Washington. Our paths soon diverged, however, as I left for the University of Washington to pursue a career in science, and Steve stayed at NU to pursue a career as a pastor. In 2012, however, our lives turned full circle as we both were back in Seattle, Steve as a lead pastor within a historic AG church and me as a science leader within NOAA Fisheries.

We still would not have connected had it not been for providential intervention. In John 10:27 Jesus says, "My sheep hear my voice, and I know them, and they follow me." Now such divine guidance may see strange to some, but like MLK saying that he "experienced the presence of the Divine ... [through] the quiet assurance of an inner voice,"[1] after months of visiting different churches in the Seattle area, my wife and I also experienced that "quiet assurance of an inner voice" directing us to attend Steve's church.

I soon became familiar with Steve's understandings of the gospel, both as a member and a church deacon. We were exposed to his life challenges through the intimacy of a small group fellowship and friendship. The more we saw, the more we realized that Steve is the real deal, practicing what he preached with an emphasis on spiritual formation. Such a focus involves the heart and is central to our faith, for "out of the abundance of the heart" (Luke 6:45) our mouths speak.

NT Wright puts it this way:

> These qualities ... [habits of the heart] are not, so to speak, "things you have to do" to earn a "reward," a "payment." Nor are they merely the "rules of conduct" laid down for new converts to follow. They are, in themselves, the signs of life, the language of life, the life of new creation, the life of new covenant, the life which Jesus came to bring.[2]

The fruit of the Spirit becomes the evidence of this new creation as a Romans 12:1-2 transformation takes place. It is the proof of the pudding that an alignment is underway so that every aspect of our life reflects Christ. It demonstrates the reality of that transformation as judged by others rather than by ourselves.

I had previously come to the same conclusion while still living in Alaska. As a new federal science manager, I had sought to incorporate my faith into my work life. I had seen how fellow believers would openly display their faith through a Scripture-laden t-shirt or a Bible strategically placed. Yet such actions seemed performative in practice and polarizing in outcome, an ineffective Christ-like witness. There had to be a better way that was appropriate for a secular workplace and the position of authority I held.

My aha moment came while reading James Kouzes and Barry Posner's, *The Leadership Challenge*—seeing their advocacy of core values for great leadership.[3] Like a light bulb coming on, I realized how the development of core values would meet my goals. Core scriptural injunctions such as Micah 6:8, Colossians 3:12-14, and the Sermon on the Mount would become operational through core values focused on virtue. Especially virtue reflective of spiritual fruit, "against which," according to Scripture, "there is no law."

It is our living that really counts, for our actions speak louder than words. As the Apostle John so clearly says, "let's not just talk about love; let's practice real love. This is the only way we'll know we're living, truly living in God's reality" (1 John 3:18-19, MSG). The Apostle Paul then chimes in, urging us to "live a life worthy of the calling you have received. Be completely humble and gentle; be patient, bearing with one another in love. Make every effort to keep the unity of the Spirit through the bond of peace" (Eph 4:1-3, NIV).

"Getting Along"

This unity stuff is a big deal, an outcome of a Christ-like nature and a core Christian virtue foundational to the calling of the church. Yet unity is on life-support today as disunity is the norm. The yeast of polarization has swept through society, with a pervasiveness even affecting the church, defiling our salt and light calling in a fallen world. This crisis in our land is really a crisis of faith which is why Steve Pecota's new book, *Getting Along: The Church's*

Quest for Unity in a Polarized World, is so timely and needed.

Steve begins his manuscript by showing why unity is central to both the Godhead and the gospel. He then shows why disunity is central to our human nature: it is both normative and unavoidable. This disconnect is a big deal, yet much of it is unknown to us despite the harm it does to the very core our faith.

Here's how that happens. We are an impressionable people influenced by the company we keep. Our yearning for community, for connecting with others, is part of our nature and hardwired within us. It causes our brain to engage in self-reflectance—to take the measure of beliefs, values, and attributes of others.

Our self-reflectance system, through its assessment of the beliefs and values of others, opens the door to an exchange of beliefs. We think that exchange goes both ways. But the force of community puts the thumb on the scale through a subversive process mostly unknown to us. Like the Trojan horse in Greek mythology, the weight of community slips through our subconscious and then takes over our identity to align our values with theirs. This new orientation, achieved through belief harmonization, fulfills our yearning to be liked, loved, and included.

With that fulfillment, however, we become new people, discipled into a new way of life. As our identity is remade, our nature becomes changed through a syncretistic mixture of conflicting kingdoms. We are what we love, and our loves tell a new story of a devotion no longer solely focused on Jesus.

This syncretistic nature blemishes our faith and changes our witness, with outcomes often inconsistent with the gospel. Here's J. D. Greear, former Southern Baptist Convention President: "Whenever the church gets in bed with politics, the church gets pregnant. And our offspring does not look like our Father in Heaven."[4]

The most destructive change arises, however, from an allegiance to our groups, creating an us-*versus*-them worldview marked by polarization. We see examples of this polarization every day in our lives. In our social media feeds, in our discourse with friends and family, and even from prominent faith leaders such as the thinly disguised declaration by Al Mohler at a highly partisan conference that it is "absolutely necessary" for all Christians to vote in the 2022 midterms and that any Christian who votes "wrongly" is being "unfaithful" to God.[5]

Hope and Hopelessness?

A sense of hopelessness exists in America over an irreconcilable state of polarization that grows deeper and wider with each passing year. Academic studies such as those by Morgan Marietta and David Barker in their book, *One Nation, Two Realities*,[6] paint a hopeless picture for an America hopelessly polarized. So do an increasing number of pundits across both sides of the aisle. Day after day, malice, distain, and outrage are amplified through the feedback loops of our echo chambers.

These academics and pundits see little relief in sight: but aren't we "His workmanship, created in Christ Jesus for good works" (Eph 2:10, NKJV)? As Marietta and

Barker and others toggle through potential solutions, they show again and again how none of these solutions show any promise: but hasn't "his divine power ... given unto us all things that pertain unto life and godliness, through the knowledge of him that hath called us to glory and virtue" (2 Pet 1:3, KJV)?

The Apostle Paul famously writes that Christ in us is "the hope of glory" (Col 1:27, NIV). Getting Christ in us is another story, though, and as Steve shows using the latest research into human neurology and behavior, it is the crux of the problem given the yeast of cultural assimilation. It is not enough to "just have a little talk with Jesus" as the quartet song of my youth proclaims. Yes, that's a critical aspect of our faith. But we need to be *spiritually formed*, and that only happens over time and with intentionality.

We need to put off to fully put on Christ. Yet we typically largely ignore this first step, thinking some magical set of words will do the job. Discipleship is a process, though, overseen by the Holy Spirit, accomplished within God's community, and facilitated by those gifted for ministry.

There Is a Way Out

Steve charts a course from hopelessness to hope by offering five discipleship-oriented solutions—all grounded in Scripture yet all immensely practical, leveraging academic research to sharpen our "putting off" with the goal of restoring the priority and practice of unity in the church. When Steve speaks about unity, these are not abstract or theoretical thoughts. He writes from experience, having—in Eugene Peterson's language—a long obedience in the same direction[7] toward the priority of unity in both ministry and faith practice. He also writes from the heart through his fidelity to right doctrine as evidenced by a faithfulness to Christ-like orthopraxy.

Steve's last three and concluding points—unity deserves the highest level of attention by spiritual leaders, unity remains exceedingly difficult to maintain, and unity requires cooperating with the Holy Spirit and with one another—need to be regarded as a first order issue of the church. We must see unity as Christ saw it—so essential that He declared it to be one of two apologetics for the reality of His mission. We must then see disunity as a fatal error, treating the current level of disunity within both society and the church as a DEFCON 1 level issue, critical to the survival to the faith and its witness to the world.

Yes, there is a way out of America's pit of despair, but it will require a renewed focus on spiritual formation that targets the polarizing spirit of this age.

The church urgently needs to hear this message, especially from pastors, teachers, and others called to lead. Yes, there is a way out of America's pit of despair, but it will require a renewed focus on spiritual formation that targets the polarizing spirit of this age. I heartily recommend Steve's book as a great place to start. You will learn about our fallen nature and how it can inflict our faith just like hypertension can afflict our body—a lethal killer that we are unaware of unless we specifically look for it. You will be presented with the centrality of unity, a nearly forgotten aspect of the faith of which there is no higher calling. And you will be challenged with the call to change, to be spiritually formed through concrete actions.

Then, just maybe then, America's healing will begin, and the hemorrhaging of believers from the church's ranks will end. This will require a church set free from its cultural bondage, though, released to exemplify what the distinguished theologian N. T. Wright calls "the church's greatest calling"[8]—unity. As the Church exemplifies such unity, it can once again, through its life witness to the emerging generations, present "the story of God bringing humankind to be the *imago Dei*, to be the reflection of the divine character, love, where we show the world what our God is like."

—Steve Ignell
Deputy Science and Research Director,
Alaska Fisheries Science Center, NOAA Fisheries (ret.)

Preface

At perhaps his most vulnerable moment, shortly before he went to the Cross, Jesus prayed for His disciples. He poured out His heart to the Father, asking that the disciples would be made pure and holy and kept safe from Satan's power. Notably, he not only prayed for the disciples, but also for those who would believe in the testimony of the apostles, that they would all be one so the world might believe that the Father had sent Jesus (John 17:21). The visible unity of the Church plays a decisive role in how the world responds to the good news.

Each generation of the Church faces unique challenges to the fulfillments of Christ's prayer, but the partisanship evidenced in the contemporary era presents an exceptional hurdle. Polarization over politics, race, and the COVID-19 pandemic has forced believers to navigate a minefield they have not previously faced. Thankfully, the Holy Spirit provides spiritual leaders with insight and character qualities to assist them in resisting this divisive spirit so they can pursue unity with believers.

This book came about as a result of my doctoral studies where I designed The Unity Project, a seminar for pastors that identified causes of disunity and encouraged activities that maintain the unity of the Spirit. During our sessions together, we examined the root causes of polarization through the lens of cognitive distortions to which every human falls prey. Specifically, I employed three metaphors for how humans form human judgment: System 1 and System 2 (Daniel Kahneman), the scout and soldier (Julia Galef), and the rider and the elephant (Jonathan Haidt). Through The Unity Project, I challenged a group of Seattle pastors to apply those metaphors to their ministry context, and I provided them with the vocabulary for speaking constructively about polarized issues with their congregations. I also called attention to the reality that in-groups not only solidify self-identity but also blind their members to the value and complexity of those outside the group.

The project participants comprised a politically, socially, and ethnically diverse group that engaged in lively discussions about the quest for unity in their churches. By examining relevant cultural artifacts and applying biblical principles for promoting unity in a partisan environment, I sought to equip these pastors to maintain the unity of the Spirit more effectively in their ministry contexts. I remain profoundly grateful for their timely and heartfelt insights into and application of the content. This book is the result of that journey and provides a resource for Christian leaders to help the church on its quest to pursue and maintain unity in a polarized world.

Acknowledgments

This book began as a doctoral project, so I extend my first thanks to those who spurred me on to launch and complete my doctoral degree. My father, Dr. Daniel Pecota, demonstrated a lifelong commitment to sound biblical scholarship and applied it to the lives of his students. My commitment to lifelong learning certainly commenced through his example. Dad taught New Testament Greek to several generations of pastors at Northwest University, and my decision to use the Greek original rather than transcribing it is a subtle nod to his influence. Dr. Steve Hayner served as my mentor during a crucial time of my ministry formation. His challenge to write down twenty-year goals first placed a doctoral degree on my goal sheet, where it remained through countless iterations until my degree completion some forty-five years later. Both of them have graduated to the Church triumphant and now enjoy the unmitigated "well done" of their Savior.

Erica Huinda served as my editor for the doctoral project. Not only did she significantly improve my writing craft, but she served as cheerleader-in-chief. Her "Please, please, please ... you've got to turn this into a book!" encouraged me to believe that God had given me something to say to a general audience. My project adviser, Dr. Earl

Creps, helped me formulate not only one but two approved project prospectuses. His guidance gave me confidence that the subjects I cared about had broad applicability for ministry.

Dr. Lois Olena, who assisted me through the project design process at AGTS, edited this work and helped me turn a somewhat technical project into a book with wider appeal.

In 2013, I invited Dr. Christena Cleveland to speak at Calvary Christian Assembly. Her messages shaped my thinking about how deeply our sense of personal identity is bound together with group membership—and just how entrenched my own racial stereotypes might be. She was ruthlessly realistic yet hopeful about changing the status quo of congregational life in the American Church. Her insights started me down the pathway and laid the groundwork for The Unity Project.

I remain indebted to Steve Ignell, whose passion to help believers resist cognitive distortions and observe principles of sound reason helped mold the outline for The Unity Project and enhanced the impact in the lives of the participants. I also express my gratitude to each of the participants in The Unity Project, who through their lively engagement and sincere desire for unity made the project a labor of true joy. They were a living demonstration of how believers with widely varying political perspectives can engage in genuinely fruitful dialogue.

I am deeply grateful for the three congregations God enabled Karen and me to serve in long-term pastorates: twelve years at Calvary Chapel, nine years at Christliche

Gemeinde Norderstedt, and twelve years at Calvary Christian Assembly. Each ministry context provided a positive illustration of "making every effort to keep the unity of the Spirit through the bond of peace" (Eph 4:3, CSB). In addition, the Marriage Encounter teams we led for sixteen years in German-speaking Europe underscored the truth that unity is at the very core of God's plan for marriage. Each ministry setting indelibly shaped my character as a spiritual leader.

Finally, I cannot begin to express how profoundly my family has shaped this endeavor. The intellectual vigor of our two children, Kevin and Kathryn, provided a superb mirror of the world and enhanced my perspective on the Church and contemporary culture. My wife Karen has become my most important sounding board, my most enduring encourager, and a delightful partner on the journey; she possesses insight far beyond what I recognized when we began our mutual path forty-two years ago. God had special plans in mind when He made us one.

Introduction

[I pray] that they may all be one, just as you, Father, are in me, and I in you, that they also may be in us, so that the world may believe that you have sent me (John 17:21).

My call to ministry was born in the spirit of "Kumbaya." I graduated from high school in 1971, having imbibed some of the spirit and energy of the '60s protest generation. I truly wanted to make a difference in the world. The one place I could not foresee that happening, however, was in Christian ministry. Even though I had grown up in the church and was active in Sunday school and in our youth group, I never thought of pastors as influencers. In my perspective, they were only mildly interesting to listen to and more than mildly out of touch. At best, I thought that becoming a medical missionary might suit me—at least then I could help people in a tangible way.

During my senior year, the Jesus People Movement began to bloom in Seattle. Swept up in the wave, my peers and I visited Christian coffee houses (a wonderful phenomenon that predated Starbucks) and attended the first Jesus music concerts to take place in our city. We were blown away—the atmosphere was electric (pun intended). Inspired, we even started a little band of our own.

Simultaneously, the Charismatic Renewal began to wield significant influence in churches throughout the city. Episcopalians, Lutherans, and Catholics reported being baptized with the Holy Spirit. Pastors from various denominations began regular meetings with each other. The Holy Spirit was drawing the people of God together!

Shortly after my high school graduation, my home church, Calvary Temple, became the venue for the first city-wide Charismatic Renewal meetings. For one week in June, I was thrilled to be one of 1,500 participants who night after night packed a building designed to hold 1,200. More impressively, I saw the leaders of Presbyterian, Episcopal, Catholic, and Lutheran churches all sitting together on the platform with my Assemblies of God pastor.

Together, they led the heterogeneous crowd in worship, heeded words of the Holy Spirit, and enjoyed a sense of unity with one another that felt so compelling to my young soul that it moved me to tears. Hippies sitting beside conservatives, the old with the young, and Jesus People draped with love beads next to nuns dressed in habits filled the church building beyond fire code limits. Many sat on the floor or in the aisles with yellow note pads in hand, packed knee to knee, intently chronicling the hour-plus messages. The biblical teaching seemed relevant in a way I had never experienced before, made all the more palpable by the infectious sense of community with my fellow believers. I was enthralled—and I was called. My sense that one could genuinely make a difference in the vocation of pastor began then and there.

Two months later, I had my first introduction to Francis Schaeffer, when I read his small treatise, *The Mark of the Christian.* His plea for unity within the body of Christ as an essential apologetic to the world convicted me deeply. He writes, "We cannot expect the world to believe that the Father sent the Son, that Jesus' claims are true, and that Christianity is true, unless the world sees some reality of the oneness of true Christians."[9] As God solidified my calling to pastoral ministry in the ensuing months, it became my lifelong goal to promote unity among Christians in whatever ministry context I found myself.

Thus, as a young pastor of an Assemblies of God church plant in Seattle, I prioritized connecting with pastors of other denominations, including asking Steve Hayner, then the college pastor at University Presbyterian Church, to be my mentor. While church planting in Germany several years later, I personally reached out to the other pastors in Norderstedt during the early stages of our planning. I knew that was particularly important because for decades, Pentecostals in Germany had been regarded as members of a sect. One of my favorite memories is that of Gunnar Urbach, pastor of the Lutheran church that was diagonally adjacent to the post office building in which our church met. During our dedication service, I mentioned that it was unfortunate that our meeting room was absent a cross. Shortly after I said that, Pastor Urbach disappeared, only to reappear a few minutes later, proudly carrying a portable cross from their building. He presented it to me with the words,

"Now you have a cross. Keep it as long as you need it. You are our brothers and sisters." I, along with many in the assembly that day, was moved to tears.

When my wife and I returned to Seattle in 2007, I actively reached out to fellow pastors in various group settings to promote community and to "carry each other's burdens" (Gal 6:2).[10] Calvary Christian Assembly became the venue for an annual gathering of North Seattle churches that brought together congregations across the denominational spectrum. Participants from other congregations often sought me out to say thanks and express, "This is our favorite Sunday of the year!" Unity shows up best in the midst of diversity.

Little did I realize, however, how desperately our country would need this message of unity in 2020—forever known as the year the COVID-19 pandemic shook the world. It would also be remembered as a year in which racial and political divisiveness seemed to hold America captive. *Unprecedented* was the word of the year, and newscasters used it with mind-numbing redundancy.[11] The proliferation of disinformation, the acrimonious nature of political discourse, the way issues of public health became politicized—all these symptoms of disunity, according to the social commentators, were unparalleled in their scope. In the words of many, the United States felt more divided in the past two years than ever before.[12]

The bone-numbing weariness caused by the pandemic also tore the hearts of pastors, especially considering the social division that crept into many churches. Notably, Christian congregants fell prey to the same partisan spirit that was gripping the popular culture. In June 2021, Michael Graham wrote,

> I regularly hear from about six dozen pastors from around the United States. Over the past year, each of them have expressed to me that they are exhausted, and I have yet to hear from a single one that they are thriving. When drilling down on these things, much of the exhaustion revolves around what we have all been intuitively feeling and objectively observing: evangelicalism is fracturing.[13]

More than the stress related to COVID-19 protocols and to the sudden transition to online services and Zoom meetings, the disunity pastors deal with rips at their souls. Graham's circle of pastors does not appear exceptional but normative. *Christianity Today* president and CEO, Timothy Dalrymple, calls attention to the same phenomenon in an editorial aptly entitled "The Splintering of the Evangelical Soul." He states that people, once united by faith, "are not merely dividing but becoming incomprehensible to one another."[14] In multiple conversations with Seattle pastors in my network of relationships, they consistently report a level of polarization within their congregations that they have never previously witnessed.

The participants in The Unity Project confirmed the sentiment. In the pre-survey I conducted with them before the project began, I posed the question "When you think about unity among Christians, what words or thoughts come to mind?" The responses included the following:

Dysfunction. The church struggles to let Christ govern our hearts when we are faced with other views of the kingdom of God, resulting in separation, isolation, and damaging behavior toward the body of Christ.

Currently I believe unity among Christians is non-existent. Our world is so polarizing that everything becomes a discussion or debate. For unity to occur we have to be able to see past the small minutia that we become stuck arguing in and look for the grander commonalities.

I think it's hard to find unity among Christians. Be it between denominational lines, theological convictions, issues of social justice, and politics, etc., it can almost be an on/off switch that can affect unity.

Essential, rarely existent, ultimately will happen.

The last response is my favorite. It's realistically pessimistic yet contains the element of hope. Hope for unity is justified because Jesus prayed for it specifically. In His high priestly prayer, Jesus prays for those who believe on Him: "that all of them may be one, Father, just as you are in me and I am in you. May they also be in us so that the world may believe that you have sent me" (John 17:21). Francis Schaeffer correctly observes that this is the "final apologetic," a decisive factor in determining whether people in the world will believe that the Father sent Jesus.[15] Our unity as Christians, or the lack of it, is that influential.

Defining what it means to "be one" can be challenging. Schaeffer notes that unity does not entail organizational oneness, nor is it merely ethereal in the sense of a mystical union.[16] Rather, the unity Jesus prays for is visible to the world and thus tangible enough to impact how people think. Unfortunately, the current propensity toward partisanship evident both within and between church communities negatively influences their witness before a watching world.

Social scientists assert that humans are hard wired for unity; we seek it, and it soothes our souls when we experience it.[17] Jesus, who holds all things together by His powerful Word, fully understood that reality. The universal longing for unity reflects the fact that God created humans in His image; He dwells in eternal and perfect unity as three persons in one. The human quest to participate in community springs forth from our nature as image bearers. On the other hand, our propensity for tribalism and us-versus-them thinking has its origins in our fallen nature. Notably, more than half of the works of the flesh listed in Galatians consist of sins directly related to party spirit and pride, which break relationships (Gal 5:19-21).

> The marked inability to engage in nuanced dialogue with one another can and must be shaped by the possibility of mutual hearing and speaking within the Church.

The marked inability to engage in nuanced dialogue with one another can and must be shaped by the possibility of mutual hearing and speaking within the Church. Just as in other areas of moral thinking and behavior, God calls the Church to model nuanced speech and respectfully voice differences of opinion that lead to a better understanding of the issues at hand and a mutually agreed upon course of action. Steven Levitsky and Daniel Ziblatt contend that the democratic endeavor absolutely depends upon two crucial moral qualities: mutual toleration and forbearance.[18] Notably, mutual toleration and forbearance are reminiscent of Paul's admonition: "Do nothing from selfish ambition or conceit, but in humility count others more significant than yourselves" (Phil 2:3). The kind of unity Christ prayed for is demonstrated in believers who are "quick to listen, slow to speak, and slow to become angry" (Jas 1:19). Those disciplines also prove foundational for democratic flourishing.

In a cultural context fraught with issues that bring disunity, how can Christians grow in the oneness Jesus desires? Are there concrete steps that they can take that will help the Church demonstrate unity before a watching world? Research by Nobel Prize winning psychologist Daniel Kahneman suggests that by understanding how our cognitive biases impact attitudes and judgments, we can reduce the polarizing effect of inaccurate thinking. Though completely escaping the influence of cognitive distortions remains impossible, people can learn how they function and thus circumvent their power.[19] Pastors are called to faithfully exegete both the Scriptures and the culture, thus rightly applying the healing word to broken humanity. But pastors, like their congregants, are subject to partisan arguments that are bulwarked by cognitive distortions. Those distortions may prevent them from acting as the agents of unity they are called to be. I propose that when pastors more accurately perceive the ways in which their minds can fool them, they will be better prepared to lead their congregations in actions that demonstrate mutual toleration and forbearance to those with whom they disagree.

Jesus understood that without unity, the world would lack an essential apologetic for placing belief in Him.

Thus, in my doctoral studies I set out on a project to promote unity in and among Seattle churches by helping pastors better understand the mechanisms by which individuals form attitudes, judgments, and decisions, including especially the cognitive distortions that lead to exaggerated partisanship. This book is the result of that pilot version of The Unity Project—it aims to motivate not only pastors and leaders but *all* Christ followers to adopt and teach the discipline of intellectual humility, thus enhancing Holy Spirit-inspired unity within the body of Christ.

The importance of unity in the church today cannot be overstated. Jesus understood that without unity, the world would lack an essential apologetic for placing belief in Him. In an era of extreme partisanship within contemporary culture, the Church must demonstrate a culture that runs contrary to that of the world—a spirit of unity. This book can equip believers in Jesus to more effectively counter divisiveness and promote unity, thereby enhancing the witness of the Church in the world.

Ω

This book is divided into four main parts—

Part One focuses on foundational biblical concepts that can help the church walk out the practical steps to getting along in a polarized world. These include the following: (1) the doctrine of *imago Dei* (Gen 1:26-27), with special emphasis on the communal nature of God's image in humankind, (2) Christ's prayer that the disciples and those who believe may be one (John 17), and (3) the events surrounding the Council of Jerusalem as a model for dealing with partisan division within the church (Acts 15), and (4) the Apostle Paul's charge to the churches to preserve unity amid diversity (Eph 4:3).

Part Two traces two moments in Church history during which the presence of unity among believers and practical service toward one's neighbor had a definitive impact upon the surrounding culture. The first relates the activities of Christians during the plagues that ravaged pre-Constantine Europe. The second describes how the outpouring of the Holy Spirit in the early twentieth century resulted in an unusual expression of interracial unity among believers.

Part Three examines studies of human cognition and decision making, with an emphasis on how cognitive distortions increase the likelihood of partisan attitudes and heightened group polarization. In this section, I introduce three metaphors that describe how humans make judgments and decisions: (1) System 1 and System 2, (2) the scout and the soldier mindsets, and (3) the elephant and the rider.

Part Four discusses current cultural realities that severely hinder the expression of unity within the Church. These include the human propensity to create ingroups and outgroups, the alarming degree of distrust in contemporary America, and the law of group polarization. It concludes with our reason for hope. I propose five practices that assist believers to "maintain the unity of the Spirit in the bond of peace" (Eph 4:3). The practices of (1) speaking to the elephant, (2) espousing intellectual humility, (3) responding with civility, (4) broadening the circle, and (5) choosing to embrace, have the potential to transform the nature of our fellowship and dramatically sharpen our witness.

When I think about the Church today, and particularly about my tribe (White, Evangelical, Pentecostal), I often feel saddened by our tolerance for misinformation, our tendency to smack a label on those whose opinions differ, and our fierce insistence that we've got it right. My profound hope remains that God will use this work to promote a renewed humility, an appreciation for nuance, and a deep hearted commitment to rooting our identity in Christ alone. Then the world will *truly* see that we are His disciples (John 13:35).

PART ONE
The Biblical Framework

Any treatise on Church unity must begin with the biblical witness. If one reads the Old and New Testaments with an eye for the topic, he or she will find that the goal of unity remains central to God's purposes for humanity as an essential component of His redemptive plan for the world. That plan begins with the harmonious relationships in the Garden, is immediately interrupted by sin, but is restored through Jesus, the Son, the one who breaks down "the dividing wall of hostility" (Eph 2:14) and to whom the twenty-four elders sing:

> Worthy are you to take the scroll
> and to open its seals,
> for you were slain, and by your blood you ransomed people for God
> *from every tribe and language and people and nation,*
> and you have made them a kingdom and priests to our God,
> and they shall reign on the earth (Rev 5:9-10, italics mine).

The extreme partisanship we experience today is no new phenomenon. The Scriptures aptly describe how factions within a community can easily slide into tribalism, with "us versus them" thinking, thwarting God's intended unity.

In Part One of this book, I examine the biblical basis for the community of God and the attitudes and activities that both promote and prevent unity among its members. I give special attention to Christ's prayer that His followers be one, "so that the world may believe that you have sent me" (John 17:21). I also introduce the Council of Jerusalem as an effective model for how Spirit-filled believers may seek unity when people's sincerely held beliefs conflict with those of others.

1

Created for Community— The *Imago Dei*

*"So God created man in his own image,
in the image of God he created him;
male and female he created them"*
(Gen 1:27).

When I attended Fuller Seminary in the 1980s, Ray Anderson taught my systematic theology courses. To this day, several elements of his teaching stand out to me. Early on in the course, he gave us a metaphor for theological reasoning based on his experience living in the northern plains of the United States. Every winter the ground would freeze, and every spring it would thaw. The thaw so softened the roads that vehicles, including tractors, would sink into the ground when they drove, creating enormous ruts. At one particularly well-worn intersection, Dr. Anderson observed a handmade sign warning travelers:

"Be careful which rut you choose ... you'll be in it for the next forty miles!" That gave me a life-long metaphor describing the human propensity for partisan thinking.

That metaphor dovetailed with a conviction that Anderson sought to impress upon us: our launching point significantly affects the landing point. He asserted that many of the moral and practical problems we face in the Church today have their origin in our faulty foundation—our misunderstanding of what it means to be created in the image of God. An essential characteristic of human image bearers is that they are created in and for relationships.

The fact that God designed us for community lies at the very core of human identity. This truth is made abundantly clear by the words of the Creator: "It is not good that the man should be alone" (Gen 2:18).[20] Human flourishing depends upon positive human interaction and every person intuitively senses this truth—it is the consequence of being made in God's image. We reflect God's essence as three in one, the eternal community of the divine Trinity. Stanley Grenz describes the impact of the relational nature of God:

> The divine image is not primarily individual, but is shared or relational ... . The God we know is the triune one, three trinitarian persons united in perfect love. Because God is "community"—the fellowship of the three persons—the creation of humankind in the divine image must be related to humans in the relationship as well. God's own character can only be mirrored by humans who love after the manner of the perfect love lying at the heart of the triune God. Only

as we live in fellowship can we show forth what God is like and as we reflect God's character—love—we also live in accordance with our own true nature and find our true identity.[21]

When God made humankind in His image as the crown of His creative activity, He did not merely create an individual; He created people in community. Karl Barth understood the essence of humanity as "man in encounter" with God and encounter with one another.[22] According to Barth, the two encounters, with God and with fellow human beings, remain inseparable; we can only discover our God given identity in the context of community.[23]

Four Characteristics of Encounter

The community enjoyed by the first couple is beautifully expressed in the following description of their interaction: "And the man and his wife were both naked and were not ashamed" (Gen 2:25). They did not experience shame before God nor with each other. Their relationships, both vertically and horizontally, remained unencumbered. Man and woman enjoyed a quality of encounter that reflected God's own being. Barth offers four descriptors of encounter as God intends it. First, being in encounter involves "[looking] the other in the eye."[24] This implies a character of openness, to see and be seen: "When one man looks the other in the eye, it takes place automatically that he lets the other look him in the eye."[25] This point reveals a psychological truth—only by making myself knowable to the other can I truly know myself.

Second, being in encounter requires "mutual speech and hearing."[26] Here Barth closely aligns with what psychologists have identified as necessary for human beings to feel understood, the practice of active listening. Eye contact is essential but only as the first step. When an individual hears a fellow human being repeat their thoughts and feelings back to them, they recognize that as authentic listening. M. Scott Peck insightfully observes that the act of true listening always exacts a cost on the listener:

> True listening, total concentration on the other, is always a manifestation of love. An essential part of true listening is the discipline of bracketing, the temporary giving up or setting aside of one's own prejudices, frames of reference and desires so as to experience as far as possible the speaker's world from the inside, stepping inside his or her shoes.[27]

Because true listening is difficult, few people practice it consistently. As Stephen Covey observed, "Most people do not listen with the intent to understand; they listen with the intent to reply."[28] In a partisan driven agenda, abundant speech takes place with little to no listening—this obviously misses the mark of God's design for the human experience.

Third, being in encounter "consists in the fact that we render mutual assistance in the act of being."[29] Barth understood each of these characteristics as a sort of upward ladder. Part of the reason that people resist seeing and being seen, or speaking and listening, is that they recognize that God ultimately calls them to live their lives for the sake of the other: "We must see and be seen, speak and listen, because to be human we must be prepared to be there for the other, to be at his disposal. We thus hesitate. We are afraid. This is too much to ask."[30] This is humankind's favorite excuse, that "too much is expected of him, that he is given too high and holy a destiny."[31] When we give up trying to flee this calling, however, then we begin to experience the fourth aspect of being in encounter, gladness: "We gladly see and are seen; we gladly speak and listen; we gladly offer assistance. This can be called the last and final step of humanity. Or, we might equally well say, this is the secret of the whole."[32]

Joy results from true unity
among God's people.

Barth thus argues that joy reflects the very heart of what it means to be human. This by no means implies that life remains free from difficulties. As he expresses above, each of the steps of encounter requires effort to overcome one's own inertia—they do not happen naturally. As individuals move into encounter with openness, careful communication, and a willingness to put another's interests before their own, the natural outcome is joy. Joy results from true unity among God's people: "Behold how good and pleasant it is when brothers dwell in unity" (Ps 133:1).

Unity and Disunity in the Hebrew Scriptures

The English word *unity* (Heb. *yachad* — יַחַד) appears one time in the Old Testament, although the concepts of harmony and disharmony in relationships are abundant. Psalm 133 vividly expresses the rich sensory feelings associated with unity, comparing it to oil running down Aaron's beard, an experience that most moderns have not shared.[33] The Israelites used the Psalm of Ascent in corporate worship as pilgrims made their way from lower elevations toward "the mountains of Zion" to celebrate one of the annual festivals. Leslie Allen notes that "the crowds in the holy city were a beautiful perspective of Israelite community, bound together not only by nationhood but by the covenant relationship as God's family."[34] Unity is an essential expression of shalom, the wellbeing and wholeness that God's covenant people may partake in.

> The Scriptures reveal not only that the covenant community should aspire to unity but how fleeting harmony can be.

The Scriptures reveal not only that the covenant community should aspire to unity but how fleeting harmony can be. Though created in the image of God, we rebelled against His authority; humanity sought to dethrone Him. As D. A. Carson observes: "The fall is not merely the breaking of some arbitrary rule. It is the rebellion of the creature against the Creator; it is the appalling commitment to try to usurp the Creator's place."[35] Idolatry is such a consequential sin because it symbolizes humanity's attempt to create God in our own image, reducing Him to human terms. The rebellion against God results in multiple alienations: from God, from self, from our fellow human beings, and from creation. These multiple alienations become embedded in culture and thus become systemic. It is crucial that we recognize both individual and corporate responsibility when considering the causes of evil and injustice in our world. The use of the word "systemic" has stirred up some controversy in contemporary discussions. David French observes that traditionally, "progressives are more apt to look for systemic failures and conservatives are more apt to find individual fault."[36] Both perspectives are justified, however. The doctrine of *imago Dei* declares that not only is each individual an image bearer, but each is also fallen. Similarly, the culture within which individuals think and act can point to the glory of God, but is also bent in a sinful direction. Carson states it well:

> Christians cannot long think about Christ and culture without reflecting on the fact that this is God's world, but that this side of the world is simultaneously resplendent with glory and awash in shame, and that every expression of human culture simultaneously discloses that we were made in God's image and shows itself to be misshaped and corroded by human rebellion against God. [37]

The very existence of human culture, itself a gift from God to help humans flourish in community, becomes an instrument that squeezes us into its misshapen mold.

Immediately following the narrative of the Fall, the Hebrew Scriptures recount the impact of misshapen human culture. Cain and Abel, the first two offspring of the newly created first couple, reveal the horrifying consequences of man trying to do things his way. The precipitating incident seems almost trivial to the modern reader: Cain and Abel both bring offerings to God; Abel's sacrifice is accepted, while Cain's is not. At the heart of the narrative is something deeper than a simple misunderstanding— Cain's sense of identity feels threatened. The narrative is thus paradigmatic for human community, and God extends assurance to Cain: "If you do well, will you not be accepted?" (Gen 4:7). Rather than heeding the invitation, Cain takes the most drastic step possible and murders his brother. Human discord enters on the most egregious scale.[38]

The Old Testament narrative attests to the possibility of unity and the likelihood of discord. God's covenant people, Israel, demonstrate a continuing pattern of fleeting moments of unity in purpose in obeying the Lord's commandments and identity as His people, followed by unfaithfulness, acrimony, power-seeking, and division. The divisiveness proved far more of a rule than an exception. Even the reign of David, Israel's most beloved king and a man after God's own heart, was fraught with infighting among his leadership circle and rebellion within his own family. Absalom's insurrection serves as a historical reminder that partisan loyalties can easily brew beneath the surface.

As the Scriptures chronicle a record of unfaithfulness, they also point to the prophetic longing for a new Kingdom grounded in righteousness and one in which God "will put [His] law in their minds and write it on their hearts" (Jer 31:33). In this Kingdom, relationships will participate in shalom. In this Kingdom, "everyone will sit under their own vine and under their own fig tree, and no one will make them afraid" (Mic 4:4). In this Kingdom, "the wolf will live with the lamb ... and a little child will lead them" (Isa 11:6). And this Kingdom will be initiated by an anointed and trustworthy leader, the Messiah. Through Him, God will fulfill the longing for genuine harmony among His people.

2

Jesus and the New Community

"The glory that you have given me I have given to them, that they may be one even as we are one, I in them and you in me, that they may become perfectly one, so that the world may know that you sent me and loved them even as you loved me" (John 17:22-23).

When seeking a model for how to deal with extreme partisanship, the Gospels provide the premier example. Jesus is the ultimate authority on building a unified community amid diversity. In this chapter, I examine how Jesus intentionally called followers from diverse backgrounds and persuasions to join His movement and then demonstrated to them how their cooperation could flourish within an atmosphere of humility and brotherly love.

Jesus emerges onto the Judean panorama when hope for unity among the people of God was at a low ebb. The Gospels reveal a spiritual, political, and sociological landscape fraught with partisanship. Pharisees, Sadducees, Zealots, Herodians, tax collectors—each name represents a differing approach to their cultural setting in which the Jewish territory was subdued by Roman rule. In Mark's narrative, Jesus declares that the long anticipated new order is breaking forth: "The time is fulfilled, and the kingdom of God is at hand; repent and believe in the gospel" (1:15). This is the good news they have waited for!

Within a relatively short period of time, Jesus assembles a group of followers who devote themselves to Him and His teaching. This new community of His disciples, however, was by no means homogenous; it was diverse enough to almost ensure tension. The motley crew even included extreme opposites—a tax collector and a Zealot. One willingly cooperates with the occupying force; the other seeks to tear it down, yet Jesus deliberately assembled this group after a night in prayer, seeking His Father's guidance. Jesus poured His heart and energy into this group. As the time drew nearer to His impending death, He increasingly focused His attention on the nascent community.

His disciples were slow to perceive the transformation that Jesus was initiating. Luke records that during their last supper together, "a dispute also arose among them, as to which of them was to be regarded as the greatest" (22:24). The tendency toward self-promotion had not been rooted out of Christ's closest companions, even after spending considerable time with Him. The immensity of Christ's final hours had been lost on the disciples. They concerned themselves with their potential promotion in the coming new Kingdom, a vivid reminder of the extent to which motivations and cultural values can blind humans.[39] Jesus, recognizing the strategic nature of the moment, applies the surgeon's knife. He cuts at the heart of "selfish ambition and vain conceit" (Phil 2:3) by showing His disciples a model of humility they will never forget.

Humility Is Foundational
for Unity

All cultures do not consistently value humility. As Andrew Lincoln observes, "Humility was an attitude that was regarded primarily negatively in the Greco-Roman world and associated with contemptible servility."[40] Christ's actions, however, turn His followers' culturally informed attitude toward humility on its head by taking on the role of a servant and washing the disciples' feet. He asks them, "Do you understand what I have done to you? You call me Teacher and Lord, and you are right, for so I am. If I then, your Lord and Teacher, have washed your feet, you also ought to wash one another's feet" (John 13:12-14). In stating this command, Jesus does not initiate a new purity regulation; rather, He challenges His followers to "have a readiness to perform the lowliest service for one another. Nothing was more menial than the washing of the feet ... . No act of service should be beneath them."[41] Jesus here defines the character of His new community.

Perhaps the reader has had the opportunity to participate in a foot washing service. The impact of such a service can feel quite powerful. Because foot washing is not an everyday aspect of our culture, however, the lesson may remain somewhat hypothetical. The point Jesus was making to His followers was that the most menial tasks ought also to belong to their personal repertoire. Jesus deliberately takes on the role of a slave and expects them to follow in that path. I am reminded of a personal experience with my father, Dr. Daniel Pecota, that served to vividly drive the same message home for me.

In September 1975, my father was invited to be one of the speakers at a college student leadership conference at Hungry Horse Bible Camp, beautifully situated just outside the west entrance of Glacier National Park. Because I was to begin my assignment as a college campus pastor later that month, I made the twelve-hour drive from Seattle along with him. I was excited to meet my new ministry peers.

When we arrived at the camp, it seemed strangely deserted. What we didn't realize at the time was that we had arrived nearly a day early. Dad mistakenly thought the camp began on Saturday morning instead of Saturday evening, and we had pulled in late Friday afternoon. In any case, the first order of business after a twelve-hour drive was to find a restroom, so I entered the largest building, Teakettle Lodge, and sought out the men's room. To my disgust, the room wreaked of excrement. The toilet in the end stall had completely overflowed, and literal chunks were lying on the floor—it was the worst case of sewer backup I had ever seen. I turned on my heels and went in search of another restroom, thinking to myself, "Why hasn't someone cleaned this up?"

After doing my business, I decided to explore the beautiful campgrounds, but after about forty-five minutes,

I began to wonder where my father might be. I returned to Teakettle Lodge, just in time to see him departing the men's room with a mop and bucket in tow. He had cleaned the mess that so disgusted me. I find it particularly noteworthy that *no one but God would have ever known he did so* unless I had happened upon him at that moment. He truly lived out Jesus's admonition: "If anyone would be first, he must be last of all and servant of all" (Mark 9:35).

A New Commandment

As their Passover meal concludes, Jesus proceeds to outline some of His most important instructions to His followers that would direct their lives after His coming ascension and glorification: He offers two statements pertaining to unity.[42] First, Jesus gives the disciples a new commandment to "love one another: just as I have loved you, you also are to love one another" (John 13:34). He follows it with the result of obedience: "By this all people will know that you are my disciples, if you have love for one another" (v. 35). Interestingly, Jesus calls this commandment new, despite the admonition in Leviticus to "love your neighbor as yourself" (19:18). The newness may lie in the art of loving: "just as I have loved you." This love goes beyond loving one's neighbor as oneself. It is self-sacrificial to the extent of "laying down one's life for his friends" (John 15:13) and marked by humility, patience, compassion, wisdom, perseverance, and selflessness.

The commandment is also new because it belongs to the New Covenant that Christ would soon institute through His own sacrifice. George Beasley-Murray asserts,

"Its newness would appear to consist in its being the Law of the new order, brought about by the redemption of God in and through Christ."[43] Jesus establishes a new order of relationship between God and humanity, and that has direct consequences for the manner in which believers treat one another. It also has direct consequences for the way in which the world perceives the Church, as Francis Schaeffer astutely observes:

> The church is to be a loving church in a dying culture ... . Jesus turns to the world and says, "I've something to say to you. On the basis of my authority, I give you a right: you may judge whether or not an individual is a Christian on the basis of the love he shows to all Christians."[44]

To put it bluntly, when Christians get caught up in disrespectful partisan wrangling with fellow believers, the world looks on and rightfully infers, "You must not be Christians at all!" While this exceptional level of judgment that Christ allots to the world feels uncomfortable, it is, in fact, a reality. A Christian's authenticity will be assessed by their outward expression of love, or lack thereof, for their fellow Christians.[45]

Jesus's Prayer and the Final Apologetic

In Jesus's prayer for His disciples and "for those who will believe in [him] through their word" (John 17:20), He makes it explicit that unity among believers is *the* essential component of the Church's witness before a watching world. He prays for those who will believe through the witness of the disciples, the Church, "that they may all be one, just as you, Father, are in me, and I in you, that they also may be in us, so that the world may believe that you have sent me" (John 17:21). Jesus raises the bar. Not only does the world judge the authenticity of individual believers by the love they have one for another, but their ability to believe the authenticity of Christ's claim as the only begotten Son of the Father rests upon the visible unity of Christ's followers. Schaeffer calls this unity the final apologetic: "We cannot expect the world to believe that the Father sent the Son, that Jesus' claims are true, and that Christianity is true, unless the world sees some reality of the oneness of true Christians."[46]

Remarkably, Jesus prays for a unity among believers that compares to the unity He enjoys with His Heavenly Father, a point He repeats twice in John 17:21 and 17:23:

> In both places we have four parts. [In verse 21] they are as follows: (1) "Father ... you are in me," (2) "I am in you," (3) "May they also be in us," (4) "so that the world may believe that you have sent me." In verse 23 these are the four parts: (1) "I in them" (2) "you in me" (3) that they may be "brought to complete unity" (4) "to let the world know that you sent me." In each case the effect of this structure is to add solemnity and emphasis.[47]

The influence this unity will have upon the watching world is essential for Christian witness.

Defining the meaning of "complete unity," however, requires a careful approach. Complete unity is not organizational oneness in the pattern that the ecumenical movement seeks to establish. Humans are simply incapable of that level of agreement unless compelled by brute force. Further, organizational unity does not touch at the core issues of the heart, since, as Schaeffer notes, "human beings can have all sorts of organizational unity but exhibit to the world no unity at all."[48]

Second, the unity Jesus prays for is not ethereal; He does not speak of the mystical union of the body of Christ. Instead, Jesus prays for visible unity that the world can observe and, as a result, become convinced of the legitimacy of Jesus's claims. Schaeffer pointedly observes:

> In the church at Antioch the Christians included Jews and Gentiles and reached all the way from Herod's foster brother to the slaves; and the naturally proud Greek Christian Gentiles of Macedonia showed a practical concern for the material needs of the Christian Jews in Jerusalem. The observable and practical love among true Christians that the world has a right to be able to observe in our day certainly should cut without reservation across such lines as language, nationalities, national frontiers, younger and older, colors of skin, levels of education and economics, accent, line of birth, the class system in any particular locality, dress, short or long hair among whites and African and non-African hairdos among blacks, the wearing of shoes and the non-wearing of shoes, cultural differentiations and the ... forms of worship.[49]

This practical and visible oneness "mirrors and participates in the oneness of Jesus with the Father."[50] The oneness

Jesus enjoys with His Father is especially applicable to the new community as it pertains to three key characteristics: identity, purpose, and perspective.

United in Identity

Jesus and the Father are one in respect to identity. Though the Nicene Creed clearly expresses the Christian conviction of one God who eternally exists as three distinct persons, the Gospel of John indicates that Jesus's identity is so closely bound to His Father that He visibly expresses the Father on earth:[51] "No one has ever seen God; the only God, who is at the Father's side, he has made him known" (1:18).[52] Irenaeus expounds on this:

> Clearly the Father is indeed invisible, of whom also the Lord said, "No one has seen God at any time." But his Word, as he himself willed it and for the benefit of those who beheld it, did show the Father's brightness and explained his purposes.[53]

In Ambrose's words, "Christ is the interpreter of the Godhead."[54] The Greek word for "make known" is ἐξηγήσατο, from which the word *exegesis* derives: "It is a suggestive thought that Christ is the 'exegesis' of the Father."[55]

Another event in Jesus's life reiterates the essence of His identity. On one occasion when the Pharisees claimed to be the true children of Abraham while confronting Jesus regarding His identity, Jesus challenges them: "If God were your Father, you would love me, for I came from God and I am here. I came not of my own accord, but he sent me" (John 8:42). Jesus calls them children of the devil, to which they retort that Jesus has a demon. Jesus then declares, "Truly, truly, I say to you, before Abraham was, I am" (8:58). In that statement, Jesus deliberately references the divine name Yahweh and applies it to himself.[56] The force of that statement was not lost upon His detractors, who immediately picked up stones to kill Him.

Jesus's sense of identity rested on the bedrock affirmation the Father gave Him: "You are my beloved Son; with you I am well pleased" (Mark 1:11). The vagaries of human opinion didn't shake Him. Likewise, the foundational source of a believer's identity lies ultimately in what God says about us: "Fear not, for I have redeemed you; I have called you by name, you are mine" (Isa 43:1). But we must never underestimate the value that we humans place on what others say about us. In our quest to discover our identity, we are quite dependent upon human voices. As Christena Cleveland observes,

> Who am I? The better question might be, Who do others think I am? because our self-concept, the part of our self that holds information pertaining to our identity, is extremely susceptible to outside influences.[57]

As we will discover in succeeding chapters, that susceptibility makes us especially vulnerable to building partisan loyalties. Because what others say about us affects us so deeply, we do whatever we can to ensure that they speak positively about us. As a result, we expend considerable energy trying to please those who we consider insiders.

If Christians are to truly reflect the unity of Jesus

and the Father, our core identity must be grounded in our mutual adoption into God's family. All other markers we use to identify ourselves, whether birth family, ethnicity, nationality, or social status, must necessarily be relegated to second order. Our first-order identity as children of God changes radically how Christ-followers respond to one another, especially when differences or disagreements arise. More than any other factor, our sense of identity will impact our behavior.

United in Purpose

Jesus makes another fascinating declaration to His detractors: "Truly, truly, I say to you, the Son can do nothing of his own accord, but only what he sees the Father doing. For whatever the Father does, that the Son does likewise" (John 5:19). In this statement, Jesus demonstrates a submission to His Father that flows out of His complete unity of purpose with Him. Theodore of Mopsuestia pointedly observes, "If he does only what he sees the Father doing, he evidently possesses perfect similarity with the Father in his action. And this would be impossible if he did not have the same power."[58] Jesus's alignment with the will of His Father results not from servile subjugation but perfect alignment of two wills.[59] Jesus's sole purpose is to bring glory to His Father; therefore, He aligns His will and purposes perfectly with that of the Father.

If believers are to become one with other believers, their first order purpose must be identical to that of Jesus—to bring glory to God. We express unity as we join together to accomplish that purpose. Sometimes that implies subordinating our will and opinions to a unified goal. Such subjugation does not indicate weakness but inner strength, strength manifested in a willingness to pursue a purpose higher than our own. This explains why working together on a project that advances the Kingdom proves exhilarating and fulfilling. It should not surprise us that our most profound experiences of unity come when we stand shoulder to shoulder with other believers doing Kingdom work that requires personal sacrifice for the good of the whole. Those experiences profoundly shape our sense of calling.

> If believers are to become one with
> other believers, their first order
> purpose must be identical to that of
> Jesus—to bring glory to God.

One such sacrificial moment left an indelible mark upon me during my college years. Northwest College sponsored a program over Thanksgiving break called "Operation Turkey." Teams were formed that spent the four-day holiday at a smaller church in the state performing basic repair projects, painting, and doing whatever the local pastor deemed helpful to their mission. The weekend culminated with the team helping to lead the host church's Sunday service. I recall the deep sense of connectedness that grew within our team because each of us was giving up our personal holiday for the greater good of the Kingdom. What some might have considered a sacrifice was in our experience a genuine privilege and source of joy.

United in Perspective

Finally, Jesus perfectly aligned with His Father's perspective, as demonstrated by John 3:16. The Father did not force His Son's submission to His purposes; Jesus submitted because He shared the same purpose, one informed by the same perspective. Their mutual love for lost humanity led them to a unified course of action: the Father sends the Son and the Son submits to being sent.

When we align themselves with God's purposes, He gives us a new way of seeing, a renewed perspective. We become "transformed through the renewing of [our] minds" (Rom 12:2). Divine insight now informs our old way of seeing; seeing others through the Father's eyes shapes attitudes and behaviors.

Living within this new perspective is not a given, however. It especially requires the activity of listening, both to the Holy Spirit and to one another. Believers gain the Father's perspective when we thoughtfully engage with their fellow believers about what the Father is doing and saying. In the words of Karl Barth, this calls for "mutual speech and hearing."[60] In the next chapter, I examine how the nascent Church practiced mutual speech and hearing at a time of stark disagreement.

3

Unity on What Basis?—
The Jerusalem Council

*"For it has seemed good to the Holy Spirit and to us to
lay on you no greater burden than these
requirements" (Acts 15:28).*

Christ's prayer for the unity of the believers would be put to the test from the very onset of the Church. Luke details the struggles for us in his second book to Theophilus. His testimony provides a clear witness to the fact that even redeemed individuals easily find issues over which they can divide. The sociological and theological differences between Jew and Gentile, or between Judean Jews and those of the Diaspora, provided the fodder for disputes that reached deep into the identity of the fledgling Church.

In his account of the Council of Jerusalem in Acts 15, Luke records the dispute and its profound ramifications. Here he attributes a notable phrase to the apostles: "It seemed good to the Holy Spirit and to us" (Acts 15:28). Those words aptly describe "mutual speech and hearing" as they lived it out in the Early Church: The interactions before, during, and after the council model unity amid strenuous differences of opinion. Acts 15 serves as a prototype for how to pursue unity in an age of extreme partisanship.

Luke relates the backstory that elicited the meeting:

> Some men ... were teaching the brothers, "Unless you are circumcised according to the custom of Moses, you cannot be saved." And after Paul and Barnabas had no small dissension and debate with them, Paul and Barnabas and some of the others were appointed to go up to Jerusalem to the apostles and the elders about this question (Acts 15:1-2).

Those at the council needed to settle a question at the center of the gospel: Was it necessary for Gentile followers of Jesus to become Jewish proselytes and accept the Jewish ritual laws in order to be saved? The answer to this question would determine the core nature of the whole missionary endeavor. It would also determine the definition of Christian identity.[61]

This life-altering conviction captivated early Jewish believers:

> They believed that Israel's God had come back in person and was now among and within the followers of Jesus. This belief had taken root, providing Jesus's followers with a strong, though controversial and dangerous, sense of identity.[62]

That identity, however, remained solidly Jewish.[63] The Early Christian community understood themselves as the fulfillment of the promises for God's new order described by their Jewish prophets. They now waited in eager expectation for the fulfillment of those promises, particularly the liberation "once and for all from the shame and scandal of Roman rule."[64] Adherence to the Torah was, without a doubt in their minds, one of the necessary criteria for liberation. Now, however, they hear reports that some in the Diaspora, who also follow Jesus, neglect to observe the Law. Wright sheds light on what Jewish believers in Jerusalem may have thought:

> The Jesus-followers in Jerusalem faced trouble from the start. Many had dispersed following the early persecution, but there was still a tight core, focused particularly on James himself. From at least the time of Stephen's killing they had been regarded as potentially subversive, disloyal to the Temple and its tradition. Now the disloyalty was showing itself in a new way; they were allied with a supposedly Jesus-related movement, out in far-flung lands, teaching Jews that they didn't have to obey the Torah![65]

For many early Jewish Christians, loyalty to the Torah delineated authentic faith in Jesus.

The Antioch Crisis— Table Fellowship Matters

Paul's account in Galatians 2:11-16 further provides background for the events leading up to the council.[66] When Peter first came to Antioch, he welcomed table fellowship with Gentile believers despite their ritual uncleanness, a perspective likely informed by his God-given vision before meeting with Cornelius. But when "certain men from James" (v. 12) arrived in Antioch, Peter pulled back from eating with the Gentiles for fear of offending those from the Jerusalem Church.[67] Peter's powerful influence persuaded other Jewish believers in Antioch, including Barnabas, to follow his lead. Wright conveys the intensity of this decision:

> The lasting shock of this moment is concentrated in Paul's use of the word "even." There is pain in that word, like someone trying to take a step on a foot with a broken bone in it. Even Barnabas! Barnabas had been with him through the joys and the trials of the mission in Galatia. They had shared everything; they had prayed and worked and celebrated and suffered side by side. They had themselves welcomed many non-Jews into the family. And now this.[68]

Paul's letter reveals that not only the circumcision requirement was at stake in the Jerusalem Council but also the issue of table fellowship. They needed to determine whether Gentile believers required ritual purity to enjoy a meal with Jewish Christ-followers and whether to continue observing kosher eating laws.

The Council in Process—Listening to the Spirit and to One Another

Luke's account of the council itself provides us with a notable pattern for dealing with strongly held conflicting points of view. To begin, the council members express a range of opinions. The most stringent party believed that loyalty to the Law required Christian converts to become

Jewish proselytes. Paul and Barnabas contended for full inclusion of Gentile believers, apart from adherence to the Law; they argued that it sufficed if believers exercised mutual respect and avoided practices particularly egregious to their Jewish brethren. The council needed to decide whether Christianity would consist of a Jewish sect that embraced Jesus as the Messiah or a mixed fellowship of all those who place faith in Jesus, regardless of ethnicity or religious background. In short, the very essence of what constitutes the gospel was at stake.

In the ensuing discussion and decision-making process, a pattern of Holy Spirit directed conflict resolution unfolds.[69] Peter, "after much discussion," rises to address the gathered assembly (Acts 15:7). Luke then likely paraphrases Peter's words, highlighting the crux of his message: God "showed that he accepted them by giving the Holy Spirit to them, just as he did to us" (v. 9). Here Peter recalls the story he had already voiced to the leaders in Jerusalem shortly after his encounter with Cornelius (11:1-18), an encounter that dramatically shaped Peter's life. Luke considered it so important that he chronicles it at length two times in Acts.

Peter reminds the assembly that God demonstrated His full Gentile acceptance when Peter visited Cornelius. Bruce observes, "Cornelius and his household had not even made an oral confession of faith when the Holy Spirit took possession of them, but God who reads the human heart, saw the faith within them."[70] If God accepted them and imparted His Spirt upon them as soon as they believed the gospel, then "why should further conditions now be imposed on them— conditions which God himself did not require?"[71]

The convincing power of a personal story is quite remarkable. With the Antioch crisis in the not-so-distant past, Peter shows unusual courage in standing up to the very group to whom he had previously shown deference. Ashish Varma astutely observes that the twin qualities of courage and humility define Peter's approach to his brethren at the council.[72] Both qualities are essential for promoting unity in times of division. His courage in the face of likely disparagement from his Jewish brethren lends authority to his conviction. Further, Peter's genuine humility reduces the perception that he poses a threat. He refuses to locate his standing before God on heritage or status, nor does he appeal to any presumed authority as the rock upon which Christ would build the church. As Ashish Varma observes, Peter's response echoes Christ's kenosis:

> [Peter] demonstrates the humility of Christ, risking rejection by his own people through identifying with Gentiles. Not considering his status as a Jew in a Council consisting of apostles and elders who were Jews a thing to be grasped, Peter took the form of the servant, humbly stepping into the shoes of the Gentiles. He even denounced his status as something insignificant to his position in Christ.[73]

Peter willingly admits to his own inability, and that of his fellow Jews, to keep the Law and casts himself solely upon the grace of the Lord Jesus. Peter's willingness to set aside racial identity as the basis for his standing before God provides a model for the contemporary church, as Varma contends: "The transgressed boundaries of Jew and Gentile in Acts 15 commend a similar step forward for Christians in a racially charged world."[74] I return to that important theme in Part Four of this book.

After Peter's address, "All the assembly fell silent, and they listened to Barnabas and Paul as they related what signs and wonders God had done through them among the Gentiles" (Acts 15:12), implying a growing sense of unanimity. Finally, James, who had become the leader in the Church in Jerusalem, concludes the argument: the event that Peter had reported to them about how God was gathering Gentiles had already been foreseen by the OT prophets. James asserts: "And with this the words of the prophets agree" (v. 15), thus emphasizing that the divine Word must interpret God's divine activity. For James, the Scriptures confirm that Gentile inclusion was God's plan all along.[75] He appeals to Amos 9:11-12 as the scriptural underpinning for this truth, and Luke intentionally cites the LXX version of the passage because that translation, unlike the Hebrew text, implies that God is reaching out to all people.[76] In short, James contends that the prophet's promised restoration of the Davidic kingship includes the hope that "the remnant of men may seek the Lord," and this now finds fulfillment in the mission to the Gentiles.

Peter's willingness to set aside racial identity as the basis for his standing before God provides a model for the contemporary Church.

James concludes with his judgment, spoken with authority as the leader of the church, that Peter's assessment is correct: God is welcoming Gentile believers into His family without requiring them to adhere to the Jewish Law. The church, therefore, "should not make it difficult for the Gentiles who are turning to the God" (Acts 15:19) by laying on them "a yoke that neither we nor our fathers have been able to bear" (v. 10). Instead, James offers four prohibitions that Gentile believers ought to observe. Joseph Fitzmyer clarifies their meaning: Gentile believers must abstain from

> (1) τῶν ἀλισγημάτων τῶν εἰδώλων "the polluted things of idols," i.e. food ritually unclean, contaminated by having been offered to idols in pagan sacrifice; (2) καὶ τῆς πορνείας, "and from fornication;" (3) καὶ τοῦ πνικτοῦ, "and from what has been strangled," i.e. meat from animals improperly or not ritually butchered, without having the blood properly drained from them; (4) καὶ τοῦ αἵματος "and from blood," i.e. eating food made from the blood of animals.[77]

Three of the restrictions specifically refer to food laws and thus apply to the Jewish sensitivities about table fellowship.[78] These prohibitions signify a step of good faith on the part of the council; while refusing to succumb to the circumcision party, they demonstrate commitment to avoiding offense. Given the long history of Israel's unfaithfulness regarding idol worship, the Jewish antipathy to meat offered in pagan sacrifices remained particularly acute. For Jews who had been taught their entire lives that whole classes of foods were unclean, this would have seemed a small price to pay for their Gentile brothers and sisters to abide by these comparatively modest restrictions.

James concludes by remarking that the Law of Moses is regularly preached in every city, which implies the Gentile cities of the Diaspora. Jews who are deeply committed to the Mosaic Law exist throughout the empire, and Gentile Christians need to do their best not to offend them. It is also possible that James says this as a nod to the Pharisaic party, implying that they need not worry about the proclamation of the Law, for Moses will continue to get his due.

The Church in One Accord

The proceedings result in a letter drafted for the Gentile believers in Antioch, which Barnabas and Paul will deliver. Luke emphasizes the unity within the assembly as they take these steps: "It has seemed good to us, having come to one accord, to choose men and send them to you with our beloved Barnabas and Paul" (Acts 15:25). Luke's use of the phrase "of one accord" indicates peaceful agreement, according to J. Lyle Story:

> For Luke, unity is essential for communal life and witness and is well expressed by one of Luke's favorite terms, "of one accord" (ὁμοθυμαδόν, 15.25). The term is found almost exclusively in Acts and … [reflects] Luke's portrait of the early Christian communities from sources that he trusts; … In Acts 15, the expression "of one accord" means that the decision and its implementation reflect harmony, peace, wholeness and agreement by all the parties concerned in the conflict.[79]

Through repetition, Luke demonstrates not only the unanimity of the apostles but also the wonderful cooperation between the human and divine evidenced in the decision-making process: "It seemed best to the apostles and elders to send" (v. 22); "it seemed best to us to send" (v. 25); "it seemed best to the Holy Spirit and to us not to burden" (v. 28).

Whether Paul agreed with the Council's ruling remains a matter of debate. A good deal of attention has been paid to the fact that Paul seems to dismiss the prohibition against eating food offered to idols when discussing the matter in his first letter to the Corinthians. There he states: "Food will not commend us to God. We are no worse off if we do not eat, and no better off if we do" (1 Cor 8:8). Some see this as evidence that Paul never did support the Jerusalem decision.[80] I prefer the point of view that Paul fully embraced the Council's edict as a practical guideline for behavior while at the same time arguing that, because of the victory of Jesus on the Cross, food does not matter.

When it came to theology, Paul always focused on the practical outcome of how Christian behavior affects a fellow believer. For him, the idols clearly had no influence over the food offered to them; therefore, they did not defile it. But believers could use that knowledge as an excuse to disregard the delicate sensibilities of a weaker individual. He charges that some members in Corinth used their knowledge that "an idol has no real existence" (1 Cor 8:4) in a manner that hurt the weaker members. Their superior knowledge puffed them up, but "love builds up" (v. 1).

Love, therefore, leads Paul to refrain from eating when he senses that doing so might cause a weaker one, who has not been enlightened by this knowledge, to stumble. Though Paul knows the truth about idols, he tempers his freedom for the sake of another: "Therefore, if food makes my brother stumble, I will never eat meat, lest I make my brother stumble" (v. 13). For the health of the body of Christ, he aligns himself with the Spirit and, when necessary, with the letter of the Apostolic decree.

The peace that resulted in the Church because the Apostles were "of one accord" provided a wonderful gift. Certainly, they understood the harmony as an expression of the eschatological hope for the new order, the very thing that the Jewish prophets had anticipated.

It becomes abundantly clear throughout this discussion that each of the principal parties, whether Peter, Paul, or James, were loyal to the written code but interpreted it through the lens of what the Spirit was doing among them. They practiced what some have called a Pentecostal hermeneutic. In trying to discern what God's will was for the congregations they led, all of them were practical in their approach. Theological fine points must be subservient to love of neighbor. Even cherished convictions must sometimes be suspended to provide entrance for the outsider. Practicing justice is more important than asserting superior insight. This pattern is foundational for attempts to promote unity in our contemporary church setting.

As Luke concludes the council narrative, he records the reception of the letter in Antioch: "When they had read it, they rejoiced because of its encouragement" (Acts 15:31). The peace that resulted in the Church because the apostles were "of one accord" provided a wonderful gift. Certainly, they understood the harmony as an expression of the eschatological hope for the new order, the very thing that the Jewish prophets had anticipated. A unified Church demonstrated that the new community was God's work. Just as Jesus had prayed, through the visible unity of the nascent Church, the world would believe that the Father had sent the Son.

Applicable Principles We Can Infer from the Council's Process

The Jerusalem Council serves as a model for how the contemporary Church may deal with intensely partisan issues. In brief, I observe seven principles for dealing with conflict when differences of opinion prevail:

1. **The council representatives listened to one another's stories.** They understood that the story God was writing in their lives revealed His purposes.

2. **Representatives of each position dialogued within the community context.** The opposing sides did not isolate themselves from each other. Thus, they gave no room for the law of group polarization to take effect (see chapter 10 for how this law functions).

3. **They listened to the Holy Spirit.** Their listening to the Spirit likely involved manifestation of the gifts of the Spirit, such as gifts of prophecy or gifts of knowledge. Clearly, they believed the Holy Spirit communicated with them in an overt manner.

4. **They looked for scriptural principles that applied to their questions.** They paid special attention to the scriptural big picture of God's plan for all of humanity, including His plan for the "outsiders" (the Gentiles).

5. **They allowed authoritative voices to speak and delineate policy.** They recognized that God had established leaders within their community and gave them appropriate deference.

6. **They looked for compromise so long as it did not detract from God's grand plan.** They tried to make it as easy on both sides as they could. For example, even though the Judaizers did not prevail, the community sought a solution that did not unnecessarily offend the delicate consciences of their Jewish brethren.

7. **They decided on and communicated clear expectations.** They intentionally sent envoys in teams to spread the word of their decision as broadly as possible. Even though the decision was bound to meet opposition, they did not flinch before the task of communicating a clear word.

These principles provide an excellent framework for dealing with the partisan issues of our day. For example, when it comes to racial disparities, the Church would benefit greatly if Christian leaders would simply take the time to observe principle number one—to listen to one another's stories. Providing a forum in which the majority race of a congregation listens to the stories of the minority groups would go a long way in provoking empathy and understanding. Luke's account in Acts 15 provides us with a sense of hope for the unity that may be fostered if we listen to the Holy Spirit and to those with whom we disagree.

Notably, however, Acts 15 both begins and ends with a reference to division. Though an ardent defender of unity among God's family, Paul, shortly after returning to Antioch, parts ways with his trusted ministry partner, Barnabas, because of a dispute over John Mark. The separation was not entirely negative. Paul and his new partner, Silas, "went through Syria and Cilicia, strengthening the churches" (Acts 15:41) and late in Paul's life, he specifically asks Timothy to bring John Mark with him "for he is very useful to me for ministry" (2 Tim 4:11). Nevertheless, the frank realism of Luke's account serves as a vivid reminder that the pursuit of unity will remain fraught. Christians can only maintain it through maximum effort with the aid of the Holy Spirit.

4

Unity in the Ministry of Paul

"I hear that when you come together as a church, there are divisions among you, and to some extent I believe it" (1 Cor 11:18, NIV).

The same passion for bringing Jew and Gentile to unity that Paul manifested in the Jerusalem Council carries through in his letters to the churches. His abiding passion is that believers would be one, and he disparages any spirit of division that harms community. He devotes some of his most spirited language to those who assault the unity that the Father intends for His family. He calls those who sow discord "false brothers," "hypocrites," "evil-workers," "dogs," and "ministers of Satan." More than half of the works of the flesh listed in Galatians directly relate to the sin of party spirit and pride that breaks relationships.[81] For Paul, partisan behavior within the Church is not only ugly and harmful—it is a sin.

Paul's condemnation of disunity applies rather directly to the contemporary Church in America. Like the Church in Corinth, we gravitate to heroes who concur with our chosen manner of thinking, seeking validation for our ideas by listening only to the like-minded. The forces attacking unity within the Church have never been merely of human origin; Paul calls them "cosmic powers over this present darkness" and "spiritual forces of evil in the heavenly places" (Eph 6:12). These forces empower human instruments to use deception as a weapon so that believers might be taken captive "by human cunning with cleverness in the techniques of deceit" (Eph 4:14, CSB). Perhaps more than any other issue in contemporary culture, the battle over truth claims lies at the heart of our divisions. When *my side* is defending the truth, and *your side* is fake news, the possibility for meaningful dialogue and thoughtful compromise disappears. Genuine cooperation remains both necessary and possible, however, because it results not through human endeavor—it is a product of the Spirit. Paul's admonition to "guard the unity of the Spirit" (Eph 4:3)—as one would guard a precious jewel that thieves are trying to steal—strikes the mark in our contemporary context just as it did in the first century.

Overcoming Party Spirit

Our propensity to form in-groups and out-groups emerges as one of the central themes of Paul's first letter to the church at Corinth: "I appeal to you, brothers, by the name of our Lord Jesus Christ, that all of you agree, and that there be no divisions among you, but that you be united in the same mind and the same judgment" (1 Cor 1:10). The young church was fraught with in-fighting over whose revelation was superior, dividing the church along party lines. Those parties associated themselves with symbolic heroes, who supposedly represented their particular theological leanings.[82] One group even laid claim to the ultimate one-upmanship, Ἐγὼ δὲ Χριστοῦ ("I am of Christ," v. 12). The exact nature of the division remains complex, though the conflict reflects the human tendency to rally around group identity, vilify the other parties, and proudly claim superiority.[83]

Paul's corrective word has obvious implications for our current environment dominated by partisan spirit. The human tendency is to become proud (puffed up) about one's own party line and to identify that party line with a particular leader who represents that point of view. In the end, personal identity becomes absorbed into group identity ("I am of Cephas" or "I am of Paul"). The positions and arguments themselves become less important than one's identification with a particular party.

Paul challenges this manner of behavior by rejecting the idea that superior wisdom brings any advantage. He contends instead that Christ sent him "to preach the gospel, and not with words of eloquent wisdom, lest the cross of Christ be emptied of its power" (v. 17). Some Christian leaders use this verse to defend an anti-intellectual approach to preaching, especially an anti-science bias. It is important, however, to note that Paul is not downplaying intellectual argument, which he is known to have wielded as a normal part of his arsenal, e.g., his reasoned dialogue with the Jews and God-fearing Greeks at Athens (Acts 17:17). Instead, he specifically resists appeals that use manipulative rhetoric—the Greek reads literally "by wisdom of speech" (οὐκ ἐν σοφίᾳ λόγου) "that nullifies the cross of Christ" (ἵνα μὴ κενωθῇ ὁ σταυρὸς τοῦ Χριστοῦ).[84]

Paul addresses several points of contention in which party spirit had raised its ugly head in the Corinthian Church: the acceptance of his authority as an apostle (chapter 4); the practice of church discipline (chapter 5); lawsuits against fellow Christians (chapter 6); the breaking of marriage bonds (chapter 7); whether eating food offered to idols is acceptable (chapter 8); divisiveness in celebrating the Lord's Supper (chapter 11); and pride and division in public worship (chapters 12-14). Each issue had two or more sides pitted against each other, and the church in Corinth was so fraught with division that it became the best-known example of disunity. Paul would have none of it. At one point, he utters in exasperation the sarcastic observation, "No doubt there *have to be* differences among you to show which of you have God's approval" (11:19, italics mine).

The fact that Paul continues to hope for them to demonstrate the spirit of Christ, despite their exaggerated divisions, offers hope that today's Church may also lay contentiousness aside. Gordon Fee offers an aptly constructed pastoral word:

> It is easy to see the urgency for a paragraph like this for the contemporary church, which not only

often experiences quarrels such as these at the local level, but also is deeply fragmented at every other level. We have church and denominations, renewal movements that all too often are broken off and become their own 'church of Christ,' and every imaginable individualistic movement and sect … . If there is any way forward, it probably lies less in structure and more in our readiness to recapture Paul's focus here—on the preaching of the cross as the great divine contradiction to our merely human ways of doing things.[85]

The humility of the Cross provides the pathway to overcome party spirit.

Unity Is God's Gift

Paul further expounds on the theme of oneness in his letter to the church in Ephesus. He urges them to be "eager to maintain the unity of the Spirit in the bonds of peace" and thereby raises the characteristic of unity to a level of utmost importance (Eph 4:3).[86] "Be eager" may be translated "make every effort," revealing an urgency easily missed in the English text. Marcus Barth brings the intensity to light:

"Take pains." It is hardly possible to render exactly the urgency contained in the underlying Greek verb. Not only haste and passion, but a full effort of the whole man is meant, involving his will, sentient, reason, physical strength, and total attitude. The imperative mood of the participle found in the Greek text excludes passivity, quietism, a wait-and-see attitude, or a diligence tempered by all deliberate speed. Yours is the initiative! Do it now! Mean it! You are to do it! I mean it!—such are the overtones in verse 3.[87]

For Paul, the most fundamental human division, the "dividing wall of hostility" (2:14), separates Jew and Gentile and prevents Gentiles from entering the promises of the covenant people. They were "without hope and without God in the world" (v. 12). But Jesus, through the sacrifice of His own body, "destroyed the barrier" and "reconciled both of them to God through the cross, by which he put to death their hostility" (vv. 14-16). Previous hostility became abolished through Christ. Even more, Christ's sacrifice makes possible the creation of something unknown in the Old Covenant: "His purpose was to create in himself one new man out of the two" (v. 15). As Lincoln notes, "In fact, Christ's purpose was nothing less than a new creation."[88]

Unity in the body of Christ thus expresses God's redemptive plan for humanity, so guarding that unity must become a consuming priority. As D. Martyn Lloyd-Jones intones,

> Our first and chief concern as Christians should be to guard and to preserve as precious, the wondrous unity of the Spirit ... . If we believe in God, we must ever feel that our first duty is to guard this unity, to preserve it at all costs, to strain every nerve and be diligent in endeavoring to keep it and manifest it.[89]

Curtis Heffelfinger makes the point personal: "Do you consider the call to guard the unity and peace of your body of believers as something you take so seriously that it gets your absolute best in terms of prayer, energy, strategy and overall commitment?"[90]

The unity in God's new creation, the body of Christ, is not only a divine possibility but a divinely established reality, a gift that the Spirit has already granted the Church. It is not incumbent upon God's people to create it but to maintain it (Eph 4:3). Timothy Lane and Paul Tripp state it well:

> In light of the great grace of God, Paul calls members of this new community to enter into relationships with their Christian brothers and sisters in humility, gentleness, patience and forbearance. He urges the church to be vigilant to keep the unity of the Spirit; he does not tell them to create it, because it is already a fact.[91]

Barth concurs: "While 'perfection' is still beyond their grasp, 'unity' is described here as a power that already embraces all of them."[92]

It is important to remember that the unity Paul calls the Church to maintain will not always be apparent to its members. Dietrich Bonhoeffer helpfully observes that fellowship with other believers is a gift from God, just as our sanctification is a gift. In the same way we don't always feel sanctified, we will not always feel unified. Nevertheless, the unity is a spiritual reality, guaranteed through God's activity and glorious because He makes it so. As Bonhoeffer observes:

> Only God knows the real state of our fellowship, of our sanctification. What may appear weak and trifling to us may be great and glorious to God. Just

as the Christian should not be constantly feeling his spiritual pulse, so, too, the Christian community has not been given to us by God for us to be constantly taking its temperature. The more thankfully we daily receive what is given to us, the more surely and steadily will fellowship increase and grow from day to day, as God pleases.[93]

There exists a wonderful circularity in God's Kingdom economy. The more we, through an act of faith, affirm unity as a gift that God has truly given us, the more we actualize that unity in our personal experience.

Unity Depends upon Speaking the Truth

Nevertheless, it is possible, even likely, that the church will fail to live within that divine reality. For that reason, believers must be on their guard against any falsehood that sows division, not allowing themselves to be "tossed to and fro by the waves and carried about by every wind of doctrine, by human cunning, by craftiness in deceitful schemes" (Eph 4:14). As the enemy of unity, falsehood prevents believers from seeing one another with eyes of patience, forbearance, and of love (v. 2).

Paul makes it clear that the perpetration of falsehoods he describes results from a deliberate and cunning effort to deceive—they are not merely misperceptions or honest mistakes. Those who speak lies are scheming to incite harm in the same way that Satan does.[94] There will always be individuals bent on manipulation of the truth to advance their own selfish ends. That is why "speaking the truth in love" serves as the necessary antidote to falsehood and as an essential component of unity (Eph 4:15). The "truth" described here almost certainly refers to the true gospel of salvation through Christ.[95] The truth of the gospel must be expressed "in love," a phrase repeated six times in this epistle. Paul implies that it is possible to speak the truth in a manner that does not build up but rather tears down—speaking the truth, not in love, but with ill intent. Such speaking of the truth opposes the unity of the Spirit and does not achieve the desired impact that "makes the body grow so that it builds itself up in love" (Eph 4:16).[96]

Unity in Diversity

While falsehood is the enemy of unity, differences are not. Humans tend to pursue sameness and unanimity because of our desire to belong. We continually measure our environment to test whether or not our behavior conforms with accepted norms. The Holy Spirit, on the other hand, stimulates unity in diversity, a unity that reflects the triune God who is three persons yet one (Eph 4:4-6). Rather than inspiring sameness, the glorified Son creates diversity through the multifaceted gifts that He makes available to the Church to bring them to maturity.[97] By "speaking the truth in love" (v. 15), we grow up into Christ—truth speaking results in health and growth, but only "when each part is working properly" (v. 16). Each part is unique, and each part is necessary for the health of the whole. Maturity manifests itself in "the unity of the faith and of the knowledge of the Son of God," in other words, in a shared corporate experience (v. 13). Maturity and unity remain explicitly bound together. That truth ought not to be lost upon contemporary Christians, many of whom associate strident denunciation of those with whom they disagree as the hallmark of maturity.

Paul illustrates the theme of unity in diversity especially as it pertains to the administration of the gifts of the Spirit in the body of Christ. In Ephesians, the gifts comprise various individuals who hold offices necessary for equipping the Church for works of ministry (Eph 4:12). Each office provides a different service to the Body, but their cumulative impact grows the Body to maturity, as evidenced in unity of the faith. In 1 Corinthians, Paul challenges the spirit of pride that led certain members of the church to exalt some gifts over others as a badge of achievement that made them superior to and independent of their church family (1 Cor 12:21). In verses 12-26, Paul's principal thesis asserts that the Body is one unit composed of a diversity of members. Gordon Fee's analysis of the chiastic structure of the opening argument in verse 12 proves helpful: "The opening sentence somewhat redundantly strikes both notes with equal force.

For just as		the *body* is one,	A	
	yet	has many *parts*		B
	and	all the *parts* though many		B'
		are one *body*,	A'	
So also is		Christ.		

Thus, the first clause (AB) strikes the note of diversity; the second (B'A') the note of unity."[98]

Paul explains that the unity of the Corinthians is firmly rooted in the work of the Spirit in their lives, an experience that they mutually share.[99] The Corinthians falsely used their experience of the Spirit as a marker to differentiate themselves from each other. Quite the contrary, God gives each one the manifestations of the Spirit (φανέρωσις τοῦ πνεύματος), not to exalt the individual gift recipients but to serve the common good (πρὸς τὸ συμφέρον, 1 Cor 12:7). In fact, through the ministry of the Spirit, the most essential barriers between human beings—race, religion, and social status—break down: "For in one Spirit we were all baptized into one body—Jews or Greeks, slaves or free—and all were made to drink of one Spirit" (v. 13).[100] Fee explains, "In Christ these old distinctions have been obliterated, not in the sense that one is no longer Jew or Greek, etc., but in the sense of their having *significance*, so as to put emphasis on what makes people *differ* from each other."[101] Fallen humanity tends to make differences the characteristics that define them and divide them, in an effort to determine identity. This results in a tribalism that diminishes those who differ. The self-seeking works of the flesh such as impatience, mean-spiritedness, envy, rudeness, boasting, and pride exacerbate and solidify those differences.

Fallen humanity tends to make differences the characteristics that define them and divide them, in an effort to determine identity.

God's *agape*, on the other hand, remains patient and kind: "It does not envy, it does not boast, it is not proud"

(1 Cor 13:4). Rather than exaggerating the differences that call attention to personal advantage, *agape* "is not self-seeking." As Paul reminds the church at Philippi, if believers have the mind of Christ, they will "in humility count others more significant than [themselves]" (Phil 2:3). The culture of the community is shaped by the selflessness of the Master.

Conclusion to Part One

Jesus's prayer "that they may all be one" (John 17:21) demonstrates the priority that God places on the unity of His Church. The promise that unity is a gift, made realizable by the power of the Holy Spirit, awakens a yearning for the "glorious church" without "spot or wrinkle" (Eph 5:27, KJV), which the Spirit is preparing for the bridegroom. Nevertheless, the Scriptures also remind the Church of the human propensity toward "selfish ambition or vain deceit" (Phil 2:3 NIV)—the sin of pride which inevitably thwarts unity. In the next section, I examine two instances in Church history that reveal both the profound positive impact of unity among God's people and how perilous that unity remains.

PART TWO
Two Historical Case Studies

The Church often has an uneasy relationship with the culture it finds itself in. After all, we are admonished: "Do not be conformed to this world" (Rom12:2). On the other hand, God's covenant people are called to "seek the welfare of the city where I have sent you into exile, and pray to the Lord on its behalf, for in its welfare you will find your welfare" (Jer 29:7). Andy Crouch correctly observes that Christians are called to be cultivators and creators:

> I wonder what we Christians are known for in the world outside our churches. Are we known as critics, consumers, copiers, condemners of culture? I'm afraid so. Why aren't we known as cultivators—people who tend and nourish what is best in human culture, who do the hard and painstaking work to preserve the best of what people before us have done? Why aren't we known as creators— people who dare to think and do something that has never been thought or done before, something that makes the world more welcoming and thrilling and beautiful?[102]

In Part Two, I examine two historical instances in which the Church, empowered by the Holy Spirit, engaged the prevailing culture in a transformational manner, thus making the world more "welcoming and thrilling and beautiful." First, I look at the powerful witness of the pre-Constantine Christians as they responded to the dual threats of persecution and plague. Then I show how the early twentieth-century Pentecostal revival served to inspire racial unity as the Holy Spirit led the participants to break with cultural norms of segregation and literally embrace brothers and sisters whose skin color differed from theirs.

5

The Experience of Community among Pre-Constantine Christians

"By this all people will know that you are my disciples, if you have love for one another" (John 13:35).

In his letters, Paul dealt extensively with the threats to the unity of the Church, both from within the Church and from without. The Christians of the first three centuries suffered considerably under persecution by Roman authorities, yet, as has often been noted, the communal integrity of early Christians had a powerful impact on the broader culture. At the close of the first century AD, when persecution of Christians had reached new levels of intensity, the Apostle John renewed the call to love one another; he was fully aware that the power of agape was essential to maintain the life of the community, especially when facing death. Therefore, he asserts that "he who does not love his brother whom he has seen cannot love God whom he has not seen. And this commandment we have from him: whoever loves God must also love his brother" (John 4:20-21). Tertullian, the early Christian historian and apologist, famously quoted the critics of the Christian movement as saying, "Behold how they love one another."[103] The community's love for fellow believers became an essential apologetic for the new faith, but beyond that, their actions, motivated by love, revitalized culture.[104]

In his work, *The Rise of Christianity*, Rodney Stark set out to determine how "a movement with a few thousand adherents at most in the first century become half the population of the empire by the fourth century."[105] He concludes that the Church behaved in a manner that revitalized culture. One concrete example of culture revitalization appeared in the young Church's willingness to care for the sick and dying during the two major epidemics that swept the continent in the first centuries of Christianity: "In the face of terrible conditions, pagan elites and their priests simply fled the cities. The only functioning social network left behind was the church, which provided basic nursing care to Christians and non-Christians alike, along with a hope that transcended death."[106]

The Bishop Dionysius wrote a letter at the height of the pandemic in 260, commending the local Christians for their sacrificial service:

Most of our brethren showed love and loyalty in not sparing themselves while helping one another, tending to the sick with no thought of danger and gladly departing this life with them after becoming infected with their disease. Many who nursed others to health died themselves, thus transferring their death to themselves ... . The heathen were the exact opposite. They pushed away those with the first signs of the disease and fled from their dearest. They even threw the half dead into the roads and treated unburied corpses like refuse in hopes of avoiding the plague of death, which, for all their efforts, was difficult to escape.[107]

These early Christians quite literally stuck together. They sacrificed as a community in the face of danger and heeded the words of the Master: "For I was hungry and you gave me food ... . I was sick and you visited me" (Matt 25:35-36) Stark determined that "conscientious nursing without any medications could cut the mortality rate by two-thirds or even more."[108] Those who survived felt enormous gratitude and were considerably more open to the faith. Andy Crouch observes, "The church would grow not just because it proclaimed hope in the face of horror but because of the cultural effects of a new approach to the sick and dying, a willingness to care for the sick even at risk of death."[109]

What Stark labels as culture "revitalization," Niebuhr calls "transformation." To use Niebuhr's taxonomy in a somewhat simplistic manner, the third century disciples did not resist the pagan Roman government in the mode of Christ against culture, nor did they retreat from the circumstances that confronted them and into ethereal spirituality in the mode of Christ above culture. They fully immersed themselves into the existing cultural milieu, and by doing servant activities motivated by love, they became the agents through which Christ transforms culture.[110]

The transformation of culture motif reminds us that the very possibility of human culture is a gift of God, albeit tainted by sin. In an age of exaggerated partisanship, believers may be tempted to consider the dominant cultural milieu as the enemy. The contemporary obsession of the Christian Right to "own the libs" may be understood as a "Christ against culture" orientation.[111] Paul reminds us, however, that, "we do not wrestle against flesh and blood, but against the rulers, against the authorities, against the cosmic powers over this present darkness, against the spiritual forces of evil in the heavenly places" (Eph 6:12). In other words, culture itself and the people who make up that culture do not pose the primary threat. The pre-Constantine Church recognized that fact and exercised Jesus's admonition to "Love your enemies, do good to those who hate you, bless those who curse you, pray for those who abuse you" (Luke 6:27-28). Rather than resisting the dominant culture by asserting power, they demonstrated a unique degree of self-sacrifice. When Christians pour themselves into culture with the tools granted to them by the Spirit, they affect genuine transformation.

6

Unity as a Characteristic of Pentecostal Revival

"And all who believed were together and had all things in common" (Acts 2:24).

I grew up in a classical Pentecostal church. Seeking "the infilling of the Holy Spirit" was central to our tradition. Our pastors encouraged us to ask the Holy Spirit to fill us and assured us that, if we just "let go and let God," the Spirit would fill our mouths with a divinely inspired prayer language. I recall countless times at the church altar, asking God to fill me with his Spirit and trying my very best to let God move my lips. I was convinced that if the Spirit truly was working in me, it would be obvious. I desperately wanted to avoid "doing it myself."

Toward the end of my teenage years, I came to realize the cooperation between the Holy Spirit and me as more dynamic than I had pictured it as a child. God doesn't simply take control of my lips; He creates a synergy between my spirit and His that not only enables me to speak in a language that I don't understand but that transforms my innermost being, conforming me to the image of His Son. One result of that transformation is that I enter a whole new dimension of relationship with my fellow Christians. In the words of my youth pastor, Bob Stone, you can't have a *right, tight* relationship with God unless you have a *right, tight* relationship with your brother.

The importance of unity as a marker of Spirit baptism should not be underestimated. In this chapter, I argue that early Pentecostal leaders understood unity between brothers and sisters of all races and social classes as an essential evidence of the baptism of the Holy Spirit.

According to William Menzies, in his history of the Assemblies of God, the Pentecostal Movement

> is characterized by the belief that the occurrence mentioned in Acts 2 on the Day of Pentecost not only signaled the birth of the Church but described an experience available to believers of all ages. The experience of an enduement with power, called the "baptism of the Holy Spirit," is believed to be evidenced by the accompanying sign of "speaking with other tongues as the Spirit gives utterance."[112]

The Day of Pentecost following Jesus's ascension marked the beginning of the new age of the Spirit, when God, in fulfillment of the words of the prophet Joel, poured out His Spirit "on all flesh" (ἐπὶ πᾶσαν σάρκα, Acts 2:17). The universality of God's activity on that day was illustrated in the fact that people from throughout the empire each heard the Spirit-baptized believers declaring the wonders of God "in his own native language" (τῇ ἰδίᾳ διαλέκτῳ ἡμῶν ἐν ᾗ ἐγεννήθημεν, 2:8). The new order of God leveled the ground, breaking down barriers of ethnicity and social status. The new age of the Spirit had not only soteriological implications, but it had sociological implications as well. Luke documents the sociology of the new community, especially emphasizing that the newly Spirit-filled believers "had all things in common" (πάντα κοινά, 2:44, 4:32).

Sociological transformation also characterized the twentieth century Pentecostal revival. Though highly concerned about doctrinal truth, the early movement did not catalyze around carefully written theological convictions.[113] Far more, it sprang out of an earnest desire to "grasp the very glory of God, and to bring it to earth."[114] Charles Parham, the leader of Bethel Bible College in Topeka, Kansas, shared the longing common among Holiness preachers of his day to determine what comprised the "Bible evidence" of the baptism of the Holy Spirit.[115] Toward the end of December 1900, he and his students concluded that speaking in other tongues was the normative sign of Spirit baptism. Parham and the students proceeded to lay hands on one another and pray for the Spirit's baptism, and the gift of tongues manifested on January 1, 1901.[116]

Five years later, a Pentecostal revival in Los Angeles would capture worldwide attention. Known by the location of the former livery stable turned mission house in which the meetings took place, the Azusa Street Revival (1906-1909) was led by William Seymour, an unpretentious African American Holiness preacher.[117] Seymour had briefly come in contact with Parham at his Houston Bible School in early 1906. Sarah Parham recorded that Seymour "received all the truths and teachings we had held from beginning" and memorized many of Parham's teachings "word for word."[118] He became convinced of Parham's doctrine that Spirit baptism was evidenced by speaking in tongues, though he did not receive Spirit baptism while at the school, perhaps in part due to Parham's prohibition of Blacks and Whites praying together at the altar.

In February 1906, Seymour moved to Los Angeles, where he began preaching that all true Christians should experience this work of the Spirit. On April 6, during a prayer meeting with a cross-section of spiritually hungry individuals in Edward Lee's home, Seymour called for a ten-day fast for revival. Three days into the fast, as Seymour preached from Acts 2:4 about Spirit baptism, "the fire came down."[119] The revival birthing the second largest movement in the Christian Church worldwide had begun.

Cecil Robeck offers four reasons that the Azusa Street story deserves telling as a central pillar in the birth of Pentecostalism. First, the revival "grew with unparalleled speed … . A small prayer meeting of some fifteen people, including children, grew into an internationally acclaimed congregation of hundreds in just three months."[120] Second, the new revival had "a profound effect on other congregations," resulting in numerous other church bodies joining the Pentecostal movement.[121] Third, the Azusa Street Mission "continues to function as the primary icon expressing the power of the worldwide Pentecostal movement."[122] It serves as the animating narrative that shapes the self-concept of Pentecostal and Charismatic spirituality to this day and "recovery of the Azusa Street 'story' can still provide a new impetus toward an encounter with God and spiritual growth."[123] Fourth, "it continues to serve as an example for its outreach to the marginalized—the poor, women, and people of color. In a day that is marred by endless racial strife and tension … it is important to hear how this one congregation attempted to live out a vision of racial and ethnic inclusion."[124]

Unity among Races as a Sign of Spirit Baptism

For observers of the day, one of the most startling outcomes of the Pentecostal movement was the interracial character of the meetings. This distinctive stood out in a culture in which a gathering of mixed races was an anomaly. Harvey Cox notes that

> racial integration and justice were not merely items on a "social action" agenda as they have become for many churches and denominations since. These ideals were theological … . [Seymour] believed that God was sending the Holy Spirit in these latter days to purge the church of its sinful man-made divisions and to present her as a spotless bride, prepared for the coming of the divine bridegroom whose descent was expected soon.[125]

Not everyone welcomed the racial integration; Charles Parham expressed his discontent early in the revival. When Seymour invited Parham to speak at the mission in September 1906, Parham reacted with dismay after observing the meetings. He largely opposed any social mixing of the races, though he did at times speak to mixed crowds, albeit separated by seating.[126] After his visit to Azusa, he charged Seymour with promoting fanaticism, but later writings reveal that the interracial mingling especially disturbed him: "I have seen meetings where all crowded together around the altar, and laying across one another like hogs, blacks and whites mingling; this should be enough to bring a blush of shame to devils, let alone angels, and yet all this was charged to the Holy Spirit."[127] In recent decades, Charles Parham's decidedly racist character has led to reluctance by some to claim him as a founder of the Pentecostal movement.[128] Sadly, the truth that "the 'color line' was washed away in the blood," which was so evident to Frank Bartleman, the White chronicler of the Azusa Revival, appears to be lost on Parham.[129] The social transformation, though alienating to some, continues to inspire today's Church, which struggles with its own racial division:

> In retrospect, the interracial character of the growing congregation on Azusa Street was indeed a kind of miracle. It was, after all, 1906, a time of growing, not diminishing, racial separation everywhere else. But many visitors reported that in the Azusa Street revival, blacks and whites and Asians and Mexicans sang and prayed together.[130]

The decidedly mixed leadership of men and women included Black and White deacons, ministers, exhorters, and healers: "What seemed to impress—or disgust—visitors most, however, was the fact that blacks and whites … embraced at the tiny altar as they wept and prayed."[131]

The idea that the washing away of the color line was a delineating characteristic of the Pentecostal revival is debated by current historians. James Goff argues that the experience of unity among the races that characterized the movement early on was too brief as to qualify for that status.[132] Indeed, by 1914, Seymour had revised the Articles of Incorporation of the Azusa Street Apostolic Faith Mission "to state that only 'people of color' could serve as bishop, vice bishop and trustees."[133] This has led some to accuse Seymour of having patently racist motivations, but Seymour's writings seem to belie that judgment: "Some of our white brethren and sisters have never left us in all the division; they have stuck to us. We love our white brothers and sisters and welcome them," he wrote.[134] Instead, the change in the charter likely stemmed from the practical and pastoral realities of being a Black leader in an integrated congregation.[135]

Seymour had experienced at least three incidences of betrayal by Caucasians whom he had trusted. Parham's unvarnished racist statements and disavowal of Seymour's leadership are one example. Another is that when Clara Lum, the early secretary of the mission and Seymour's close confidant, moved to Portland to join Florence Crawford, another early leader in the Azusa Street Mission, she took the mailing list of the ministry with her, practically stealing Seymour's extended ministry influence and source of potential support. Finally, William Durham, who Seymour invited to share his pulpit, began preaching his "Finished Work of Calvary" view of sanctification, in direct contradiction to Seymour's Wesleyan view, which effectively split the congregation. These experiences justified Seymour's concern that White ministers might resort to legal means to take over the mission.[136]

Seymour's disappointment with untrustworthy fellow ministers may have influenced his understanding of the biblical evidence for Spirit baptism. As the revival progressed, "Seymour concluded that tongues was only one of several important evidences of a Spirit-filled life, the chief of which were divine love, the fruit of the Spirit— and tellingly—how one treated fellow believers."[137] Some may view Seymour's de-emphasis on tongues as a point of departure from classical Pentecostalism. In view of Seymour's continuing encouragement of the gift of tongues in the life of the church, however, this does not seem to be the case.[138] Rather, the corrections that Seymour proffered to the excesses and misconceptions he observed are akin to pastoral concerns of his contemporaries. For example, J. R. Flower, an early leader of the Assemblies of God, offered similar cautions:

> Too much stress on speaking in tongues as the Bible evidence weakens the argument. To insist that this is the only evidence of the baptism in the Holy Spirit is to compel us to accept that all speaking in tongues is divine … . Let us not stress any gift or doctrine out of due proportion. Let us preach the Word and leave

the rest to God. When the Comforter comes, He will make Himself known, and evidence His presence.[139]

Though Assemblies of God doctrine identifies speaking in tongues as the initial physical evidence of Spirit baptism, it concurs that tongues alone remains insufficient.

Early Pentecostalism and Ecumenism

Seymour understood that the Spirit baptism had a powerful, liberating impact on the life of the church, one that also broke through denominational divisions. In November 1906, Seymour wrote: "So many people today are controlled by men. Their salvation reaches out no further than the boundary line of human creeds, but praise God for freedom in the Spirit."[140] The Spirit was liberating God's Church from human-made barriers as demonstrated in the unity of corporate worship. Seymour understood that tongues could be heavenly anthems and saw them as an important part of the worship experience. He writes: "Many times we do not need these song books of earth… we have no need of organs or pianos, for the Holy Ghost plays the piano in all our hearts. It is so sweet. It is heaven below."[141] Dale Irvin makes the interesting observation that speaking in tongues had a "uniquely creedal function" for the revival.[142] Ancient creeds were rejected on the grounds that they had led to human divisions in the Church, but now Christ was uniting His Body and His words, spoken through the Spirit, bringing His Church together around a central theme of Christ's imminent return.[143]

Azusa Street demonstrates that when God pours out His Spirit on all flesh, national, ethnic, and social barriers must necessarily fall and Paul's words to the Galatians become concrete: "There is neither Jew nor Greek, there is neither slave nor free, there is no male and female, for you are all one in Christ Jesus" (Gal 3:28). As Irvin notes, "For the community depicted in the book of Acts no less than for the community on Azusa Street in 1906, the baptismal experience of speaking in other tongues as given by the Holy Spirit encompassed the unity of the church because it first encompassed the unity of humankind."[144]

Still, the racial and ecumenical unity of the revival proved uneven and short lived. Leaders disagreed about the nature of sanctification and the baptismal formula. No unified voice of Pentecostal doctrine and practice emerged, and the movement split into a patchwork of various churches and associations. By 1914, "dissention and disunity seemed... rampant."[145] Many believed that a move to bring about organizational unity was the best hope of conserving the revival. Others insisted that efforts to organize would signal the death of the dynamic leadership given directly by the Spirit of God. Some warned that human organization would simply open the door for scheming men to take control. The shifting winds of opinion swirled when a call was issued for Pentecostal ministers to gather in Hot Springs, Arkansas. The organizers foremost desired to establish effective leadership, but concerns about the racial makeup of the fledgling movement was likely a motivating factor for the gathering, as well.

In 1914, many of the Pentecostal clergy held ordination credentials with the Church of God in Christ (COGIC), which in 1907 became the first Pentecostal association of churches to legally incorporate. COGIC originated as an association of Black Holiness congregations, led by Charles Mason. After Mason visited Azusa Street and received the Spirit baptism in 1907, he led the churches in his care to formally incorporate as a Pentecostal denomination. Because legal incorporation afforded member pastors certain privileges, not the least of which was a clergy discount on rail passage, the loosely connected Pentecostal pastors and churches found it advantageous to come under Mason's umbrella. However, Robeck observes, "What now seems quite apparent is that while these white ministers received ordination from the Church of God in Christ, they continued to function along segregated lines. For them, it was a marriage of convenience, not an integrated fellowship."[146] When the call came in April 1914 for Pentecostal ministers to come together for a general assembly of the Church of God in Christ in Hot Springs, Arkansas, "the mailing list was virtually all white and largely southern."[147] Bishop Mason attended the assembly and spoke his blessing over the new organization of churches, but when the assembly drew to a close, the ministers' roster of the newly minted Assemblies of God was exclusively White.

One must be careful in ascribing motive to the founding members of the new denomination. To accuse them of personal racism is not justified, although most likely some of them shared the pronounced racist tendencies of

Charles Parham. Far more likely, these individuals were pragmatic in their approach. The Jim Crow South made it virtually impossible to run an integrated organization and abide by the rules of the state. Racism was baked into the system. In this situation, as is so often the case, theological conviction gave way to current cultural practice.

This chapter in the history of the Church demonstrates the reality that God's people, filled with the Holy Spirit, can create a culture that transcends contemporary norms. Against all odds, the Pentecostal revival shaped congregations into models of unity that included unprecedented racial integration. Regrettably, the narrative also reminds us just how powerfully the dominant cultural norms influence behavior. Sadly, the celebration of unity that characterized the early days of the revival did not last. "One token of the Lord's coming is that He is melting all races and nations together, and they are filled with the power and glory of God," the *Apostolic Faith* announced in November 1906.[148] Within a few short years, the surrounding culture of racial segregation had squeezed the movement back into the predominant social norm.[149]

Conclusion to Part Two

As we observed with the pre-Constantine Church, the reality of visible unity among the people of God and the expression of sacrificial love results in exceptional fruit before a watching world. It should fill us with hope for what can be. Nevertheless, the arrogance and dominance of tribal thinking among Christians proves disturbingly resilient. In the word of the prophet Jeremiah, "The heart is deceitful above all things, and desperately sick; who can understand it?" (Jer 17:9). The Church must remain vigilant against its sway. In the following chapters, we will examine how the human brain makes judgments and why insider thinking is so stubbornly persistent.

PART THREE
Lessons From Social Psychology

Modern studies of human behavior confirm what the Scriptures assert about the human condition—human beings are intensely social creatures and profoundly unaware of their own weaknesses. As social creatures, we devote much of our cognitive processes to maneuvering our social world.

In Part Three, I introduce three metaphors that illustrate how the mind negotiates the social context: slow thinking versus fast thinking, the scout mentality versus the soldier mentality, and the rider versus the elephant. Interestingly, the three metaphors fit into the framework for behavior offered by the Apostle James: "Let every person be quick to hear, slow to speak, slow to anger" (James 1:19). In "quick to hear," I see a similarity to what Julia Galef calls the scout mentality. "Slow to speak" reminds us of Daniel Kahneman's observation that thinking can be both fast and slow, but slow thinking is more likely to produce an accurate judgment. And "slow to anger" relates to the emotionally driven intuition that Jonathan Haidt likes to call the elephant.

These three metaphors will help us identify the predictable cognitive distortions we fall prey to and how we may avoid those errors in judgment.

7

Human Brains Are Hardwired for Relationships

"It is not good that the man should be alone" (Gen 2:18).

The doctrine of *imago Dei* declares that when God created us in His own image, He designed us for relationship. Just as He exists in eternal relationship as three in one, God stamped our capacity for connection into our nature. Therefore, when relationships break down, we suffer harm at the deepest level. As I observed in Part One, the relationships God envisioned for those created in His image transcend mere casual or superficial contact. The possibilities for both joy and sorrow in our relational world are extremely vast. In the core of our being, we recognize this fact. Our greatest elations and most profound pains are tied to our connection or non-connection to God and to our fellow human beings.

Readers may discover echoes of their own experience in the following story. When I was in eighth grade, one of the more influential boys in my church youth group decided that I didn't belong anymore. He had the idea that I had eyes for the same girl he liked (in actuality, I was so shy, I could barely muster up a "hello" to her). Because of his social capital, however, he was able to turn the rest of the group against me. In what felt like hours, my church went from a place of warmth and acceptance to coolness and mockery. I recall one evening when I sat in the back seat of our family car, trying to hide my tears as my parents dropped me off for youth group—they couldn't understand why I didn't want to go inside, and I couldn't explain it to them.

My sense of alienation culminated on a youth retreat to the Twin Harbors State Park on the Pacific coast. After dinner, we had built a fire in the sand dunes and were goofing around in typical teenage fashion. At that time, there was a well-known television jingle promoting the *Campfire Girls* that had the words, "Sing around the campfire, join the *Campfire Girls*." Suddenly, before I could register what was happening, what seemed like the entire group of boys circled around me and began to intone: "Sing around Pecota, join the Pecota girls. We sing around Pecota, to watch him pick his nose." It wasn't quite on par with what Piggy endured in *The Lord of the Flies*, but it felt pretty close.

When I ask those who were present (and who are now my adult friends) what they remember about that day, they can barely recall the incident. But the fact that it is so indelibly printed upon my brain demonstrates a simple truth—our sense of wellbeing is integrally tied to what others think of us.

The rapidly evolving field of brain science has conclusively demonstrated that humans are hardwired to think about other people. PET (positron emission tomography) studies reveal that when we do not focus on anything in particular—when the brain is in neutral, so to speak—our minds do not go blank. Instead, we default to social cognition. We inherently think about "other people, oneself, and the relation of oneself to other people."[150] Above all other motivations, humans long to belong.

Matthew Liebermann contends that we do not think so much about the social world because we find it interesting. Rather, we find it interesting precisely because our brains inherently think about relationships: "I now believe we are interested in the social world because we are built to turn on the default network during our free time."[151] Humans are fine-tuned to be socially aware: "The default network directs us to think about other people's minds—their thoughts, feelings, and goals."[152]

In contrast to the traditional hierarchy of needs as Maslow asserted, Lieberman does not see physical and safety needs as the most basic for human functioning. Rather, our social needs stand in the forefront. Babies have no ability to procure food and water and protection on their own; they wholly depend upon others, for "without social support, infants will never survive to become adults who can provide for themselves. Being socially connected is a need with a capital N."[153]

Fascinatingly, MRI scans demonstrate that social pain and physical pain both light up the same areas of the human brain. In fact, the graphs of physical pain and social pain, such as the sense of abandonment or the feeling of being left out when others play a game, appear so similarly, scientists have difficulty telling them apart. Matthew Lieberman and Naomi Eisenberger studied the dACC (dorsal anterior cingulate cortex), an area more developed in humans than other mammals and particularly associated with pain reception.[154] They measured the activity of the dACC while participants played a game called Cyberball, a digital game of catch between three participants.

In the beginning, each player passed the ball to the other players in equal distribution, but gradually players B and C began to ignore player A and only pass the ball to each other. In reality, unbeknown to player A, B and C were not human players but a computer algorithm programmed to ignore player A. Although the game was essentially meaningless, the study demonstrated that player A experienced real pain equivalent to physical discomfort as a result of feeling pushed out of what they presumed to be a social interaction. Lieberman concludes, "Here, the mammalian need to recognize social threats appears to have hijacked the physical pain system to do what the pain system always does—remind us when there is a threat to one of our basic needs."[155] In other words, brain studies confirm what poets and song writers have known since time immemorial: we are inherently social beings, and relationships, or the absence of them, cause us both tangible joy and tangible pain.

We are hard-wired to focus on social relationships. The human brain exercises a variety of mechanisms to negotiate the social world and social psychology labors to identify those mechanisms. In the following chapters I introduce three metaphors for cognition that especially aid our understanding of how we make judgments about our world and the other persons in it.

First Metaphor—
System 1 and System 2

"Let every person be … slow to speak" (Jas 1:19).

As humans constantly monitor their physical, mental, and relational environment, they expend a tremendous amount of energy. Nobel Prize winner, Daniel Kahneman, observes,

> The nervous system consumes more glucose than most other parts of the body, and effortful mental activity appears to be especially expensive in the currency of glucose. When you are actively involved in difficult cognitive reasoning or engaged in a task that requires self-control, your blood glucose level drops. The effect is analogous to a runner who draws down glucose stored in her muscles during a sprint. [156]

Desiring to know how humans regulate their energy output when making judgements and decisions, Kahneman and his research partner, Amos Tversky, sought to determine how rational and calculating humans are when forming opinions or taking action. They first met at a conference at which Tversky presented a paper asserting that humans were quite rational in their approaches to decision making, almost as if they were amateur statisticians. Danny listened attentively to the presentation and responded after the lecture, "Brilliant talk, but I don't believe a word of it."[157] This interaction began a collaboration that ultimately changed the way the world thinks about thinking.

Eventually, their combined research would go on to demonstrate that "human beings hardly behave as if they were trained or intuitive statisticians. Rather, their judgments and decisions deviate in identifiable ways from idealized economic models."[158] Most importantly for their groundbreaking work in behavioral economics, Kahneman and Tversky illustrate how the digressions from perfect rationality follow set patterns and that "errors are not only common but also predictable."[159]

One underlying cause of faulty judgments stems from the human tendency to be cognitive misers; we do not exert more brain energy than we need. Christena Cleveland explains,

> The human brain is limited in its ability to pay attention to and process information; the volume of information to which we are exposed on a daily basis far exceeds the brain's ability to process it. To cope with this imbalance, we become cognitive misers, conserving our mental energy by selectively choosing what we'll pay attention to, using mental shortcuts

(like categorizing) and avoiding situations that demand a lot of cognitive resources.[160]

Kahneman and Tversky describe this phenomenon by using the metaphor of two distinct but interdependent cognitive systems. System 1 employs intuitive thinking; it operates "automatically and quickly, with little or no effort and no sense of voluntary control."[161] System 2, on the other hand, "allocates attention to the effortful mental activities that demand it, including complex computations. The operations of System 2 are often associated with the subjective experience of agency, choice, and concentration."[162] System 2 entails slow thinking; it goes into action when the issue at hand requires mental effort beyond the quick and automatic activity of System 1.

Retrieving the answer to 2+2, for example, employs System 1; the answer to 17x24, on the other hand, requires deliberate mental effort. If one makes the effort to actually do the math, "the computation was not only an event in your mind; your body was also involved. Your muscles tensed up, your blood pressure rose, and your heart rate increased."[163] A careful observer would note that your pupils dilated during the whole deliberative process, then quickly shrank again as soon as you came up with the answer or gave up.

We tend to see ourselves as primarily driven by System 2, consciously weighing the evidence and employing a set of beliefs to sort through issues and problems. However, because System 2 requires significant effort, people tend to avoid it when possible. System 1 suffices for most normal day to day functioning. For example, we effortlessly react to the unevenness of a sidewalk on which we walk; we assess the potential stability of a chair with a mere glance; we identify without deliberation a certain cloud formation as indicative of rain; or we instantaneously and unconsciously analyze the potential threat of a stranger coming our way.[164] System 1 sorts through stored data in the brain according to a coherent story and stimulates an appropriate response. Impressions, intuitions, and feelings dominate. Coherence is key; the brain defaults to interpreting the data in a way that makes sense.

Because System 1 works so effectively, we universally rely on it more than we should. Determined to create a coherent story, we tend to ignore holes in the data that, upon more deliberate reflection, might lead to a different conclusion.

That truth is demonstrated through three simple thought exercises that Kahneman and Tversky administered to their students:

- A bat and ball cost $1.10. The bat costs one dollar more than the ball. How much does the ball cost? 5 cents or 10 cents?

- If it takes 5 machines 5 minutes to make 5 widgets, how long would it take 100 machines to make 100 widgets? 5 minutes or 100 minutes?

- In a lake, there is a patch of lily pads. Every day, the patch doubles in size. If it takes 48 days for the patch to cover the entire lake, how long would it take for the patch to cover half of the lake? 24 days or 47 days?[165]

Take a moment to note your answer before looking at the endnote.[166]

The danger hidden behind this simple exercise is that we put great stock in conclusions that *feel* right, whether they are correct or not. For example, Kahneman and Tversky discovered that we are susceptible to the *anchoring effect.* Anchoring "occurs when people consider a particular value for an unknown quantity before estimating that quantity."[167] They once did an experiment in which they asked students at the University of Oregon to estimate the percentage of African nations that were members of the United Nations. Before asking them the question, however, they had them spin a "wheel of fortune" that was marked with numbers between 0 and 100. The wheel was in fact rigged so that it only stopped at 10 or 65. After spinning the wheel, the professor instructed the small group of students to write down the number. Then he asked the students two questions: "Is the percentage of African nations among UN members larger or smaller than the number you just wrote? What is your best guess of the percentage of African nations in the UN?"[168] The number on the wheel obviously had no bearing upon the answer and the students should have ignored it. "But they did not ignore it. The average estimates of those who saw 10 and 65 were 25% and 45%, respectively."[169]

It is perhaps not surprising that anchoring is effective. Anyone who has bargained for a purchase in a Middle Eastern market is aware of how much the starting figure impacts the ultimate outcome. What ought to shock us is that a number with absolutely no relationship to the subject could have such a profound impact on the outcome. We think of ourselves as rational decision makers, but in fact we are influenced by multiple factors that have nothing to do with reason.

Humans are storytelling animals who gather various bits of information and try to make sense of them. When we hear a phrase or statement, our default is to assume that it has meaning, and we try make sense of it by fitting the information into the story. But we are easily led astray. As Kahneman observes, "System 1 understands sentences by trying to make them true, and the selective activation of compatible thoughts produces a family of systematic errors that make us gullible and prone to believe too strongly whatever we believe."[170] System 1 helps us to effectively navigate our environment, but it also has severe deficiencies—it requires System 2 to provide appropriate balance.

Heuristics: Mental Shortcuts

Kahneman and Tversky identified several mental shortcuts that System 1 regularly employs to arrive at conclusions. They call the shortcuts heuristics, from the Greek word *heuriskein*, meaning to "find out" and "discover": "The technical definition of heuristic is a simple procedure that helps find adequate, though often imperfect, answers to difficult questions."[171] Early in their research, they turned their attention to two often utilized heuristics: representativeness and availability.

Representativeness

Representativeness is the tendency for people to make judgments by comparing "whatever they are judging to some model in their minds. How much do those clouds resemble my mental model of an approaching storm? How closely does this ulcer resemble my mental model of a malignant cancer?"[172] The closer the item observed resembles my mental model, the more likely I am to assign it to that category. The problem with representativeness is not that it works poorly but that it works too well. Because conclusions based upon representativeness often prove correct, we tend to rely on them even when the data may not justify the assessment.

Representativeness comes into play, for example, in the judgment of whether another person poses a threat. Recent examples of police killings of Black men have brought this issue to national attention. Many ask why more Black men are victims of police shootings than their White counterparts when encountering law enforcement. Studies have demonstrated that others judge people with Black faces as considerably more threatening than those with White faces. One group of researchers "asked people to rate the height, weight, and strength of young black and white men from photographs showing only their faces. Study participants consistently rated black men as taller, heavier, and stronger than white men."[173]

Another study asked White college students to view a video of two students involved in a discussion that suddenly gets heated to the extent that one physically pushes the other. The researcher found

> striking differences based on race. When the person doing the shoving was black and the victim was white, 75 percent of the participants rated the behavior as "violent." But when the person doing the shoving was white and the victim was black, only 17 percent of the students considered that same behavior "violent." In fact, 42 percent of whites who shoved blacks were deemed to be simply "playing around"—but only 6 percent of blacks who shoved whites were categorized in that benign light.[174]

Participants frequently perceived the behavior of Black students as violent when the identical action by White students was understood as harmless banter.[175]

Availability

Another factor that dramatically impacts System 1 is the availability heuristic: the propensity to judge the frequency of an event based upon how readily examples come to mind.[176] For example, we tend to avoid flying immediately after a serious air crash occurs. We judge flying as more dangerous because the example of the crash is readily available. We perceive memorable incidents as probable. Conversely, we judge the unremarkable as improbable.

This heuristic helps us navigate a world full of risks, but it can easily lead to significant miscalculations. It also impacts how we assess causality. As storytelling beings, we search for the why. The human mind focuses so intently on building coherent stories that it will snatch the closest available information that seems relevant. A readily available coherent story will likely hold sway over other alternatives, even when the proposed explanation is unlikely. As Kahneman observes, "A remarkable aspect of your mental life is that you are rarely stumped."[177]

A Machine for Jumping to Conclusions

Because System 1 seeks coherence and works quickly, it remains particularly susceptible to jumping to conclusions. Once the mind settles upon a particular explanation, our brains readily continue down that pathway, filling in the details as we go. But this may lead to significant miscalculations. Kahneman states:

> Jumping to conclusions is efficient if the conclusions are likely to be correct and the costs of an occasional mistake acceptable, and if the jump saves much time and effort. Jumping to conclusions is risky when the situation is unfamiliar, the stakes are high, and there is no time to collect more information.[178]

The judgment errors we make, known as cognitive distortions, fall into several common categories. One of the most common is confirmation bias.

Confirmation Bias

In our attempt to build coherent stories of the world around us, we show a strong preference for voices that confirm our preconceptions. Kahneman expresses this tendency well:

> Contrary to the rules of philosophers of science, who advise testing hypotheses by trying to refute them, people (and scientists, quite often) seek data that are likely to be compatible with the beliefs they currently hold. The confirmatory bias of System 1 favors uncritical acceptance of suggestions and exaggeration of the likelihood of extreme and improbable events.[179]

The lazy System 1 prefers to create coherent stories without the messiness of checking for information that might disprove the preferred conclusion.

Confirmation bias, a well-known phenomenon in today's media environment, is made more likely due to the information silos propagated through cable news and social media. Both legal and technological factors have intensified the polarized nature of broadcast media. In 1934, Congress passed the Communications Act, which created the bipartisan Federal Communications Commission. The act introduced the fairness doctrine, requiring radio and TV broadcasters to present both sides of controversial matters of public interest. In 1987, during the Reagan presidency, the FCC abolished it.[180] Conservatives had long contended that public media, overall, leaned left, necessitating counterbalancing voices. In 1988, Rush Limbaugh became one of the first to take advantage of the new media landscape in a nationally syndicated talk radio program that featured Limbaugh's distinctively provocative style. This gave rise to a plethora of boisterous talk radio shows that intentionally propagate right- or left-wing views. The listener could pick their own poison, so to speak, without the bothersome invasiveness of a balancing voice. Cable news followed suite: Fox News and MSNBC, both founded in 1996 in the post-fairness doctrine era, incorporated their ideological leanings into their brand identities.

The advent of social media, particularly Facebook (2004), YouTube (2005), and Twitter (2006), provided a new technology for presenting one-sided news content. Programmers specifically designed the algorithms in Facebook and YouTube to keep users online by suggesting further content they might find interesting. Because the algorithms suggest similar content, users experience the well-documented rabbit hole effect in which algorithms propel readers to click on websites that represent a similar point of view to what they have already read.

Studies demonstrate that the propensity to rely on ideologically oriented news sources contributes significantly to the "law of group polarization."[181] Those who identify with a particular party "categorize news outlets into in- or out-group outlets much like they categorize people into either in- or out-groups based on their party affiliation."[182] The in-group bias not only leads them to selectively consume news from the preferred organization but "to perceive news as biased when it is attributed to an outlet with a reputation of supporting an opposing party—regardless of the news content."[183]

In one study, participants read identical news reports that were then (falsely) attributed to news sources known to have left or right leanings. Participants attributed significantly more bias to the reportage from sources they labeled as an outgroup. The authors note that, sadly, "Pre-existing skepticism may render fruitless the journalistic effort to be fair and balanced in reporting. Widely held beliefs regarding conservative or liberal media bias may have gained momentum to the extent that the preconception of (not actual) bias in news may color the interpretation of the news."[184]

The tendency toward group polarization occurs especially when groups of like-minded individuals come together to discuss political topics. Cass Sunstein notes that when people have the opportunity to discuss current issues of concern with members of their ingroup, their perceptions of the issue narrow rather than broaden:

> When people talk together, what happens? Do group members compromise? Do they move toward the middle of the tendencies of their individual members? The answer is now clear, and it is not what intuition would suggest: Groups go to extremes. More precisely, members of a deliberating group usually end up at a more extreme position in the same general direction as their inclinations before deliberation began.[185]

It appears that discussion in groups has a negative impact on human judgment, particularly when the group is comprised of members predisposed in a similar direction. This result is not encouraging. Later in the book I introduce a more hopeful aspect of group deliberation, but suffice it to say, *in-group* deliberations alone do not tend to further the quest for truth.

In-Group Bias

Like confirmation bias, in-group bias limits our capacity to make balanced judgments. In-group bias leads us to give preferential treatment to others whom we consider as members of our own group, including the tendency to infer outsized authority to their opinions. As Christena Cleveland observes, "The simple act of using us/them distinctions leads us to prefer us over them."[186] The distortion goes further, however. Not only do we prefer the opinions of our ingroup, but we also minimize the complexity and nuance represented in the outgroup:

> When we categorize, not only do we draw a very clear line between those who are like us and those who are not like us, but we also tend to think that all of the people who are not like us are the same. It's not just that they are all different from us; they are all different in the same way. The fancy name for this tendency is the outgroup homogeneity effect. On the one hand, we tend to view the outgroup as homogenous: "They are all the same." On the other hand, we tend to view our ingroup as heterogeneous: "We are all unique."[187]

Unfortunately, this results in a loss of motivation to interact with outsiders; insiders falsely assume "they already know everything there is to know about them."[188] The group polarization effect becomes even more exaggerated.

WYSIATI

Kahneman identified another cognitive pattern that discourages thoughtful deliberation and encourages jumping to conclusions: WYSIATI (what you see is all there is). The human mind works exclusively with available information and makes judgments based upon its limited knowledge, mostly ignoring the reality that more and differing information may exist. Kahneman observes,

> Information that is not retrieved (even unconsciously) from memory might as well not exist … . The measure of success for System 1 is the coherence of the story it manages to create. The amount and quality of the data on which the story is based are largely irrelevant. When information is scarce, which is a common occurrence, System 1 operates as a machine for jumping to conclusions.[189]

Thus, the impact of WYSIATI has profound implications for human behavior and social functioning. In its effort to make sense of the world, the intuitive system ignores the existence of the information of which it is unaware.

Botched Drone Strike: A Case Study about Cognitive Distortions

When I led The Unity Project with pastors in Seattle, I used current news stories as discussion fodder for discovering how cognitive distortions impact decision making. One account we discussed was the drone strike that took place in Kabul in late August 2021.

During the chaotic days of the fall of Kabul to Taliban forces, a particularly deadly suicide bomber attack at the Hamid Karzai International Airport on August 26, 2021, took the lives of at least 183 people, including thirteen U.S. service members. The U.S. command went into a heightened degree of alert, suspecting similar attacks would follow. On the ground, intelligence indicated that a white Toyota Corolla was likely to be involved in an immanent strike. On the morning of August 29, Reaper drone surveillance observed the driver of a white Corolla picking up an object at a compound suspected to be an ISIS safehouse. They continued to surveil the driver, noting that he made several stops that seemed suspicious, including dropping off several jugs at one compound, then returning later in the day and loading several containers of what was judged to be bomb making material into the trunk of his vehicle. Just before 5 p.m., the sedan made its final stop in a small courtyard near a busy street about two miles from the airport. Drone operators observed as the driver interacted with one other man in the courtyard and judged that a strike at that time was least likely to involve further casualties. After asking questions to validate the attack, the ground force commander, General Donahue, concurred. The drone command launched a single Hellfire missile that stuck the target in less than a minute. "Seconds after the missile was launched, the drone operators could see on the grainy live-video feed that other figures—most likely children—were approaching the sedan. But it was too late to stop the strike."[190]

On closer examination after the strike, the driver of the vehicle turned out to be Zemari Ahmadi, a worker for a California-based aid group, Nutrition and Education International. Ahmadi's early morning stop at the presumed ISIS safe house was actually his boss's home, where he picked up a computer. The military later acknowledged that the safe house may have been in one of the nearby buildings rather than the location they surveilled. Ahmadi's stop to drop off jugs was the headquarters of the aid group, but that information was unknown to the strike team. And the objects that he loaded into the sedan later in the afternoon were likely water canisters, cargo that Ahmadi regularly transported because of water shortages in the city. The courtyard in which his vehicle was struck belonged to one of Ahmadi's relatives, the uncle of several of the children who were stuck. In all, ten civilians lost their lives, including seven children.

In a press conference on September 17, General McKenzie conceded, "It was a mistake, and I offer my sincere apology."[191]

In view of the human capacity to construct stories in order to explain data, the outcome should not surprise us. Before you read on, take a few moments to analyze the decision-making process of the drone team and commander. What cognitive distortions played a role?

———————————

All of the biases we have examined thus far played a role in the incident. *Confirmation bias* ensured that once the initial call was made to surveille the Corolla that stopped at the presumed safe house, all of Ahmadi's subsequent activities appeared suspicious, even though his movements were completely in keeping with his job responsibilities.

In-group bias limited the information flow that the team was receiving; they trusted their sources concerning the location of the safe house and the make and model of the sedan that was to be used. Alternative scenarios or the likelihood that the data could be inaccurate were not given appropriate consideration.

WYSIATI prevented the drone team from looking at the bigger picture and, ultimately, provided them with the green light to make the strike. They saw no children in the courtyard; therefore, there must be no children there.

Other biases also played a role. *Probability neglect* led the team to disregard the low probability that they had the right "white Toyota Corolla"—Corollas being far and above the most common vehicles in Kabul.[192] In addition, the *halo effect*, whereby one data point is extrapolated to imply connection or causality, likely played a role. The mere proximity to the airport of the spot where the Corolla stopped and an object was picked up was deemed significant. Though proximity to the airport was one aspect of the reported threat, that fact taken by itself was statistically insignificant because it equally applied to many thousands of houses. Nevertheless, that data point served to further confirm the overall narrative the drone team created. In the end, because the story they told themselves was internally consistent, it became convincing—this despite the fact that every assumption the team made about Ahmadi and his vehicle was fiction.

In sum, the human brain efficiently makes quick judgments based upon heuristics that aid intuition. Those same shortcuts can also lead to failures in judgment of which the subject may be unaware. As Kahneman notes, all too often System 2 fails to intervene:

> Self-criticism is one of the functions of System 2. In the context of attitudes, however, System 2 is more of an apologist for the emotions of System 1 than a critic of those emotions— an endorser rather than an enforcer. Its search for information and arguments is mostly constrained to information that is consistent with existing beliefs, not with an intention to examine them.[193]

We pride ourselves on being rational decision makers, but on our own we are largely unable to recognize the powerful influence of our subconscious intuitive system. A Christian will not be surprised by this fact. The Scriptures are replete with admonitions to be cognizant (the KJV expression is "take heed"), to think before we act, to be "slow to speak" (James 1:19). In short, the writers of Scripture well understood the difference between the impulsive System 1 and the deliberative System 2. Danny and Amos's research echoed the biblical tradition. Christ followers in today's polarized political environment ought to take heed and do the same.

9

Second Metaphor—The Scout and the Soldier Mindsets

"Let every person be quick to listen" (Jas 1:19).

In **The Scout Mindset,** Julia Galef studies the human tendency to resist new information that conflicts with existing preconceptions. She offers another metaphor that helps us understand how we make judgments and decisions by contrasting the soldier and the scout mindsets. According to Galef, a soldier endeavors to defend the status quo, to hold onto territory—their quest for information is directionally motivated. Because the soldier deems any change in the status quo as a threat, the soldier will fend off evidence that contradicts cherished beliefs. When confronted with contradicting evidence, the soldier will ask, "Must I believe it?"[194] The bar for accepting new information is high because new information might threaten established beliefs. When offered evidence that confirms the status quo, the soldier will ask, "Can I believe it?"[195] The soldier exhibits a low level of resistance to confirmatory information.

The bar for accepting new information
is high because new information might
threaten established beliefs.

Galef submits that the scout mindset provides a more productive pathway to process information. A scout does not primarily seek to protect the status quo but the accuracy of the map: "If directionally motivated reasoning is like being a soldier fighting off threatening evidence, accuracy motivated reasoning is like being a scout forming a map of the strategic landscape."[196] When confronted with new information, the scout will ask, "Is it true?" Reasoning is like mapmaking; therefore, in the scout mindset, "there's no such thing as a 'threat' to your beliefs. If you find out you were wrong about something, great—you've improved your map, and that can only help you."[197]

No one is 100 percent soldier or 100 percent scout, nor is a soldier mindset purely negative. Protection of one's property, one's group, and one's belief system is both necessary and desired. Galef notes,

> We use motivated reasoning not because we don't know any better, but because we're trying to protect things that are vitally important to us—our ability to feel good about our lives and ourselves, our motivation to try hard things and stick with them, our ability to

look good and persuade, and our acceptance in our communities.[198]

A soldier mindset is often necessary to promote and protect morale within a group. In start-up businesses, for example, promoting morale may require the leader to deliberately blind oneself to the very limited likelihood of success.[199]

Because a soldier mindset interprets data in a manner favorable to one's own interests, we ought to view its conclusions with a degree of skepticism. A soldier mindset serves to protect and enhance personal ego. This is demonstrated, for example, in the way people respond to questions about personal wealth. Galef observes, "Poorer people are more likely to believe that luck plays a big role in life, while wealthier people tend to credit hard work and talent alone."[200] In reality, both luck and hard work significantly factor in accumulating wealth. The defensive soldier mentality, however, tends to search for conclusions that place the individual in the best light. If a person is poor, it serves their ego to believe that wealth is largely due to good fortune. If a person is rich, the conviction that wealth results from personal diligence is most flattering.[201]

Soldiers also tend to overemphasize immediate rewards rather than pursuing the long-term benefits that come from truth seeking, resulting in self-sabotage: "The source of this self-sabotage is present bias, a feature of our intuitive decision-making in which we care too much about short-term consequences and too little about long-term consequences."[202] An often-unrecognized benefit of the scout mentality is long-term improved cognitive skills. Even when the issue an individual grapples with has no obvious personal impact,

> the way you think still impacts you indirectly because you're reinforcing general habits of thought. Every time you say, "Oh, that's a good point, I hadn't thought of that," it gets a little bit easier for you to acknowledge good points in general.[203]

If for no other reason, we should aspire to be scouts because the scout mindset will make us smarter!

Directionally Motivated Reasoning in the Current Political Environment

As I began converting my doctoral project into this book, the January 6 Select Committee began conducting public hearings. The perceptive reader will have recognized that many of the principles discussed in this work have direct application to America's fraught political environment. The primary thrust of this book is intentionally apolitical. Nevertheless, because the charge that the election was stolen presents a major source of disunity within the contemporary church, I believe it would be disingenuous if I did not address the issue directly. At the risk of alienating some readers with whom I dearly want to stay in dialogue, I assert that former President Trump's persistence in promoting the stolen election narrative and the persistence of so many evangelicals in believing his claim is a clear illustration of directionally motivated reasoning.

During his public testimony under oath, former Attorney General Bill Barr testified that every time Barr dismissed or refuted a false election fraud claim, Trump would introduce another. Barr stated:

> There was an avalanche of all these allegations of fraud that built up over a number of days and it was like trying to play whack-a-mole … . All the early claims that I understood were completely bogus and silly and usually based on complete misinformation.[204]

The former president was motivated to believe that fraud occurred and therefore actively sought the next theory once Barr set one aside. I submit that, in response to Barr's criticism of each fraud claim, Trump's inherent response was "Must I believe that?" But in regard to the further theories that corresponded with his assertion of election fraud, Trump's mindset was, "Can I believe that?"

The events leading up to January 6, 2021, include the infamously contentious six-hour December 18, 2020 White House meeting that included Rudy Giuliani, Sidney Powell, and Michael Flynn, along with a number of White House staff. The sworn testimony about that meeting demonstrates Trump's propensity to latch onto bizarre theories that supported the premise of a stolen election.

The beleaguered staffers, including White House Council Patrick Cipallone, tried desperately to convince the president to make a fact-based judgment, but Trump leaned heavily into the arguments that aligned with his wishes. He scoured the Internet for corroboration. Richard Donoghue, former acting deputy attorney general, testified that in one conversation with the president, Donoghue was trying to convince him that the allegation about Italian satellites changing voting machine tallies from Trump to Biden was "pure insanity." Trump countered that there must be something to it. "You guys may not be following the Internet the way I do," Trump purportedly stated.[205]

Trump's persistent directionally motivated reasoning ought not to surprise us—in fact we ought to find it familiar. It is not enigmatic to Trump in particular but to human beings generally. We all want to preserve what is comfortable, well-known, and serves our personal benefit. However, the soldier mindset becomes problematic when it is not balanced by a genuine curiosity about the truth.

The Necessity of Curiosity

Life is exceedingly complex, and how we respond to each challenge depends upon a variety of factors. The scout mentality can assist us to navigate confusion, but more importantly, it can help us make peace with it. Kahneman observes that System 1 does not do well with confusion—it will try to fill in the gaps with whatever bits of information it can muster, trying to build a coherent story.[206] Galef, however, encourages readers to lean in to confusion: "Leaning in to confusion is about inverting the way you're used to seeing the world. Instead of dismissing observations that contradict your theories, get curious about them."[207] When someone operates according to an existing map and encounters territory that does not fit the map, they tend to dismiss contradictions, but that curtails learning. As an essential quality, curiosity drives the scout to form a more accurate understanding of the world by grappling with contradictions.

During the days of the COVID-19 lockdown, the Apple TV series *Ted Lasso* struck a note of optimism that millions of viewers found remarkably refreshing. The series follows the unlikely premise that an American football coach, Ted Lasso, is called to coach a Premier League Soccer club in Manchester. My favorite moment in season one was when Ted's nemesis, Rupert Mannion (the former club owner), challenges Ted to a round of darts and Ted accepts, only after upping the wager to the extremely high stakes of awarding Rupert key coaching decisions for the soccer club for the rest of the season. The other characters, including Rebecca, the current owner of the team and Rupert's ex-wife, are aghast. As the match progresses, Ted is seemingly doomed to certain defeat, needing two triple 20's and a bullseye to win. He then begins a monologue about curiosity:

> You know, Rupert, guys have underestimated me my entire life. And for years, I never understood why. It used to really bother me. But then one day, I was driving my little boy to school and I saw this quote by Walt Whitman, and it was painted on the wall there. It said, "Be curious, not judgmental." I like that.

Ted throws a dart and hits his first triple 20.

> So I get back in my car and I'm driving to work, and all of a sudden it hits me. All them fellas that used to belittle me, not a single one of them were curious. You

know, they thought they had everything all figured out. So they judged everything, and they judged everyone. And I realized that they were underestimating me … . Who I was had nothing to do with it, 'cause if they were curious, they would've asked questions. You know? Like, "Have you played a lot of darts, Ted?"

Ted throws another dart and hits his second triple 20.

To which I would've answered, "Yes, sir. Every Sunday afternoon at a sports bar with my father, from age 10 until I was 16, when he passed away."

There is a pregnant pause. Then Ted declares, "Barbecue sauce" and confidently tosses the third dare and hits the bullseye. The crowd erupts into wild cheers. Ted adds casually, "Good game, Rupert."[208]

Not only is this clip the ultimate example of an underdog defeating a bully, but it also teaches so effectively that curiosity is central to a balanced life. Galef concurs—curiosity is at the very heart of the scout mentality.

Moving toward a Scout Mentality

One might argue that any reasonable person ought to readily adopt the scout mentality; however, individuals have extreme difficulty detecting their own motivated reasoning. People believe themselves to be scouts, but their behavior denies it. Galef explains, "Feeling reasonable, being smart and knowledgeable, being aware of motivated reasoning—all these things seem like they should be indicators of scout mindset, yet they have surprisingly little to do with it. The only real sign of a scout is whether you act like one."[209] She identifies five behaviors that indicate a scout mindset:

- Telling other people when you realize they were right
- Being open to personal criticism and acting upon it
- Voluntarily proving yourself wrong
- Actively taking precautions to avoid fooling yourself
- Cultivating relationships with good critics[210]

Given that standard, few individuals exemplify the scout mentality. None of us particularly enjoys criticism or being proved wrong, not to mention proving ourselves wrong! It takes real fortitude to seek out contrary voices. Galef quips, "It's tempting to view your critics as mean-spirited, ill-informed, or unreasonable. And it's likely that some of them are. But it's unlikely that all of them are."[211] So we must persist in fostering friendships with those who are unlike us, just as President Lincoln famously built a cabinet that one author dubbed "a team of rivals."[212]

The desire to practice the scout's behavior serves as the first qualification for becoming one. Your curiosity, combined with good friends who are willing to be good critics, will place you on the pathway toward the scout mindset.

10

Third Metaphor—
The Rider and the Elephant

"Let every person be … slow to anger" (Jas 1:19).

As demonstrated in the last chapter, the dispro-
portionate leverage that intuition wields in human
cognition hinders drawing an accurate map of the
territory. Jonathan Haidt addresses this theme in his
book, *The Righteous Mind.* As a social psychologist and
moral philosopher, Haidt is particularly concerned with
moral judgments—not just why we do the things we do
but why we think we are right to do those things.[213]
He contends that we engage in moral reasoning not
primarily for ourselves but for others. When seeking
a reason to not do something, a simple "I don't want
to" suffices as a subjective rationale, but we find that
unsatisfactory. According to Haidt, "We do moral

reasoning not to reconstruct the actual reasons why we ourselves came to a judgment; we reason to find the best possible reasons why somebody else ought to join us in our judgment."[214]

Haidt observes that early social psychology fixated on the tension between reason and feelings. The broad swath of Western culture encouraged people to make moral judgments based upon reason apart from emotions. The thought was that people will be better members of society if their moral decisions are cerebral. More recent research has demonstrated that separating feelings from reason is a false dichotomy. Instead, "moral judgment is a cognitive process, as are all forms of judgment. The crucial distinction is really between two different kinds of cognition: intuition and reasoning."[215] Our intuitions tend to be more influenced by the emotional aspect of our being. As Kahneman and Tversky demonstrate, the intuitive aspect of human moral reasoning predominates over conscious decision making. Haidt uses the metaphor of an elephant (intuition) and a rider (reasoning) to describe the relationship between reason and intuition. He asserts that

> The mind is divided, like a rider on an elephant, and the rider's job is to serve the elephant. The rider is our conscious reasoning—the stream of words and images of which we are fully aware. The elephant is the other 99 percent of our mental processes—the ones that occur outside of awareness but that actually govern most of our behavior. [216]

Just as an elephant is overwhelmingly more powerful than the rider who seeks to control it, intuition is the dominant player when it comes to our moral reasoning.

Like Kahneman, Haidt asserts that information overwhelms us, making it impossible to think through every situation. Our brains intuitively turn to known stories to make sense of the world. They do so quickly and intuitively. Intuition behaves with considerable force; as the rider submits to the dictates of the elephant, reason follows where intuition goes. The rider is not merely passive, however:

> The rider ... can see further into the future (because we can examine alternative scenarios in our heads) and therefore it can help the elephant make better decisions in the present. It can learn new skills and master new technologies, which can be deployed to help the elephant reach its goals and sidestep disasters. And, most important, the rider acts as the spokesman for the elephant, even though it doesn't necessarily know what the elephant is really thinking. The rider is skilled at fabricating post hoc explanations for whatever the elephant has just done and is good at finding reasons to justify whatever the elephant wants to do next.[217]

The rider is skilled at rationalizing, an especially useful trait when it comes to defending one's moral behavior.

As the metaphor implies, intuition drives most moral choices, which remain largely unconscious. A deliberated action simply feels right or wrong—the elephant plods along its preferred pathway. The pathway is not arbitrary, however. Moral intuition always develops within a social context, especially that of our family and close circle of friendships. Patricia Churchland observes, "Moral values ground a life that is a social life. At the root of human moral practices are the social desires; most fundamentally, these involve attachment to family members, care for friends, the need to belong."[218] In other words, our social environment powerfully influences ethical decision making.[219]

People are both inherently selfish and "groupish." Haidt explains, "We love to join teams, clubs, leagues and fraternities. We take on group identities and work shoulder to shoulder with strangers toward common goals so enthusiastically that it seems as if our minds were designed for teamwork."[220] The groups that we belong to bind us to each other, giving us both a sense of purpose and identity; however, they also blind us to the perspectives of outsiders and to our own shortsightedness. In short, we find ourselves bound to our groups and largely blind to the power that our own moral intuition wields over us:

> Morality binds and blinds. It binds us into ideological teams that fight each other as though the fate of the world depended on our side winning each battle. It blinds us to the fact that each team is composed of good people who have something important to say.[221]

Because our sense of identity is so closely tied together with our social networks, we tend naturally to prefer and defend our own tribe. We also resist any effort from outside to change our moral point of view, particularly if that effort takes place on a rational level.

Most of us attempt moral persuasion by means of rational argument. To use Haidt's metaphor, my rider tries to convince your rider that my side is right. I assert the superiority of my moral point of view, using sound paradigms and logic to make the point. My opponent, with their own set of paradigms and conclusions, does not budge. That is because our elephants (our subconscious intuition) dictate the starting and ending points. If the elephants remain unmoved, the rider won't go anywhere, either. Haidt asserts that "if you want to change people's minds, you've got to talk to their elephants."[222] In other words, you must communicate in such a way as to address their base level intuitions.

When I led The Unity Project with a group of pastors in Seattle, I assigned each participant to read Dr. Martin Luther King's *Letter from Birmingham Jail*.[223] For the participants, this piece proved to be the most moving cultural artifact that we studied. We unanimously reached the conclusion that Dr. King was a master at "talking to the elephant."

In April 1963, Dr. King led a march of Black protesters in Birmingham without a permit and was subsequently jailed. The letter he wrote from that jail cell was his response to an article in *The Birmingham News* written by eight moderate White clergymen, expressing their concern that Dr. King's nonviolent protest contradicted the scriptural admonition: "Submit yourselves for the Lord's sake to every human authority" (1 Pet 2:13, NIV).

They argued that progress was indeed taking place, and true believers ought to patiently wait for God to change the attitudes and actions of the officials in charge.

Dr. King first began penning his response in the margins of the newspaper article. The contents were eventually smuggled out with the help of his lawyer, transcribed, and printed by several news publications. The letter became a centerpiece of the civil rights movement and a moving tribute to King's ability to influence human perception.

Letter from Birmingham Jail serves as a powerful illustration of how one can constructively engage with those who disagree with them, in short, how to connect with your opponent on the intuitive level and address their elephant. To begin, from the onset of his letter, King was careful to build a bridge with his opponents by acknowledging their best intentions. He writes: "But since I feel that you are men of genuine good will and that your criticisms are sincerely set forth, I want to try to answer your statement in what I hope will be patient and reasonable terms."

King proceeds to carefully chronicle the history of non-violent protest in Birmingham, a city where "there have been more unsolved bombings of Negro homes and churches...than in any other city in the nation." He refuses to ignore the charge that he was coming into Birmingham as an "outside agitator." Instead, he defends his right to be there, arguing: "Anyone who lives inside the United States can never be considered an outsider anywhere within its bounds" and "Injustice anywhere is a threat to justice everywhere." King's example reveals that talking to the elephant does not mean avoiding issues of conflict—King addresses the problem directly. What he does not do is berate the people he is addressing.

King is also careful to find areas that he had in common with his opponents. For example, he appeals to the biblical tradition that was so familiar to the readers of his letter—he sidles his elephant next to theirs:

> Just as the prophets of the eighth century b.c. left their villages and carried their "thus saith the Lord" far beyond the boundaries of their home towns, and just as the Apostle Paul left his village of Tarsus and carried the gospel of Jesus Christ to the far corners of the Greco-Roman world, so am I compelled to carry the gospel of freedom beyond my own home town. Like Paul, I must constantly respond to the Macedonian call for aid.

The biblical image of "God's call" most certainly spoke to the personal experience of his fellow clergymen.

King also deliberately shares the story of segregation using strong emotional images, thus eliciting the empathy of his fellow pastors. With descriptive language on par with the best in literature, he pulls them into the arc of the Black experience:

> Perhaps it is easy for those who have never felt the stinging darts of segregation to say, "Wait." But when you have seen vicious mobs lynch your mothers and fathers at will and drown your sisters and brothers at whim; when you have seen hate-filled policemen curse, kick and even kill your black brothers and

sisters; when you see the vast majority of your twenty million Negro brothers smothering in an airtight cage of poverty in the midst of an affluent society; when you suddenly find your tongue twisted and your speech stammering as you seek to explain to your six-year-old daughter why she can't go to the public amusement park that has just been advertised on television, and see tears welling up in her eyes when she is told that Funtown is closed to colored children, and see ominous clouds of inferiority beginning to form in her little mental sky, and see her beginning to distort her personality by developing an unconscious bitterness toward white people; when you have to concoct an answer for a five-year-old son who is asking: "Daddy, why do white people treat colored people so mean?"; when you take a cross-country drive and find it necessary to sleep night after night in the uncomfortable corners of your automobile because no motel will accept you; when you are humiliated day in and day out by nagging signs reading "white" and "colored"; when your first name becomes "nigger," your middle name becomes "boy" (however old you are) and your last name becomes "John," and your wife and mother are never given the respected title "Mrs."; when you are harried by day and haunted by night by the fact that you are a Negro, living constantly at tiptoe stance, never quite knowing what to expect next, and are plagued with inner fears and outer resentments; when you are forever fighting a degenerating sense of "nobodiness"—then you will understand why we find it difficult to wait.

I confess, every time I read those words, they bring tears to my eyes. What parent can read King's account without being moved? And that was exactly Dr. King's intent—he wanted White pastors like me to feel what it is like in his world. Fifty-nine years later, he speaks to my elephant.

There are countless other examples throughout the letter of how Dr. King challenges the perceptions of his White colleagues without demeaning them. He masterfully draws upon their shared worldview to point to the fact that Jesus demands more from his Church than to sit and wait. In another masterful paragraph toward the end of the letter, King again points to their shared history and invites his fellow pastors to join him in following Christ's call:

> But though I was initially disappointed at being categorized as an extremist, as I continued to think about the matter, I gradually gained a measure of satisfaction from the label. Was not Jesus an extremist for love: "Love your enemies, bless them that curse you, do good to them that hate you, and pray for them which despitefully use you, and persecute you." Was not Amos an extremist for justice: "Let justice roll down like waters and righteousness like an ever-flowing stream." Was not Paul an extremist for the Christian gospel: "I bear in my body the marks of the Lord Jesus." Was not Martin Luther an extremist: "Here I stand; I cannot do otherwise, so help me God." And John Bunyan: "I will stay in jail to the end of my days before I make a butchery of my conscience." And Abraham Lincoln: "This nation cannot survive half slave and half free." And Thomas Jefferson: "We hold these truths to be self evident, that all men are created equal ..." So the question is not whether we

will be extremists, but what kind of extremists we will be. Will we be extremists for hate or for love? Will we be extremists for the preservation of injustice or for the extension of justice?

Dr. King reminds his White colleagues that they are part of the same tradition, but to avoid extremism, it was possible that they might miss the challenge Christ was calling them to. He extends an invitation, saying in effect, "Join me as I join this long succession of extremist predecessors. We are part of the same team in our calling to promote liberty and justice."

Almost sixty years later, Dr. King's words demonstrate that it is possible to speak truthfully, passionately, and compellingly to others with whom we disagree. Moral persuasion, though difficult, can produce results. Although the groups to which we belong bind and blind us, their influence need not remain impermeable.

PART FOUR
How Should We Then Live?

Part Three introduced the three metaphors as a tool to help us think differently. The metaphors have several things in common. They all contend that our social nature serves as the key to understanding what motivates behavior. Each emphasizes that human intuition dictates much of human decision making. Each also demonstrates that we derive our sense of identity from the groups to which we belong. Our self-concept is inherently group oriented. Because of that fact, we are particularly susceptible to organizing our social relationships into groups of *us* and *them*. One of our most dominant felt needs is to belong.

In **Part Four**, I examine the current cultural realities that severely hinder the expression of unity within the Church. My hope is that as we learn to more carefully examine our cognitive distortions and biases, we will grow to exercise a scout mentality, seeking truth even when the truth we discover is uncomfortable and disrupts the status quo.

In chapter 11, I explore the first factor that provokes disunity—the human propensity to create ingroups and outgroups. In this chapter, I include some stories from my own life that demonstrate how readily we fall into that pattern.

In chapter 12, I address a second factor that provokes disunity by calling attention to the alarming degree of distrust that contemporary Americans demonstrate toward their government and their fellow citizens.

In chapter 13, I turn to the third factor that provokes disunity, the tendency, especially exacerbated in our internet age, for people to selectively pick their sources of information. This is demonstrated in an increased distrust of expert testimony and the propensity for groups that share similar beliefs to push one another toward more extreme views rather than mediating the immoderations.

Chapter 14 begins to bring the book to its conclusion by providing a hopeful but realistic pathway forward. Based on the research on cognitive processes covered in Part Three, I propose five practices that can significantly change the unity landscape within the Church, thus dramatically enhancing her witness. The practices consist of speaking to the elephant, demonstrating intellectual humility, practicing civility, broadening one's circle, and choosing to embrace. Just as Paul views unity as normative when he challenges believers to maintain the unity of the Spirit" (Eph 4:3), these practices are the natural outgrowth of Holy Spirit's work in the Church. They should not be viewed as exceptional, but as normative. Nevertheless, because each practice requires "counting others more significant than yourselves" (Phil 2:3), the practices are indeed extraordinary when compared to normative human behavior in a fallen world, hence their power to bear witness to Christ's authority—"so that the world may believe that you have sent me" (John 17:21).

Finally, I conclude with three central implications for unity that all believers ought to carefully consider.

Factor #1 That Provokes Disunity: Ingroups and Outgroups

"There is neither Jew nor Greek, there is neither slave nor free, there is no male and female, for you are all one in Christ Jesus" (Gal 3:28).

I became keenly aware of the emotional reward associated with belonging during our eighteen years as missionaries in Hamburg, Germany. The rituals and rites of passage associated with group membership stood out in stark contrast because our membership was not automatic. We celebrated every experience in which we were treated "just like a German" as a small triumph.

One of the requirements that expatriates least enjoy is the annual trip to the *Auslanderamt* (office of registration). Each year, we would show up at our appointment time and stand in the dingy hallway of the aging, grey building with a group of other foreigners, each waiting for their name to be called. Eventually we would be called in to sit in front of an official whose desk stood directly adjacent to another official who serviced another family at the same time. That meant we heard every bit of the conversation that took place right next to us—no privacy concerns here!

After one year in the country, Karen and I rode the subway downtown to fulfill the annual ritual. Our German had improved significantly since our first visit one month after our arrival, but we were at best still novices in the language. On this occasion, a Turkish family was seated at the desk next to us. It didn't require much discernment to recognize that the measure of respect afforded to these fellow aliens did not match the respect we were given. The official was rude, impatient, and mocking. Admittedly, our German was perhaps a bit more fluid than theirs. And we did have the appropriate paperwork filled out. But it became clear that the principal reason for the difference in treatment was our skin color. We were just as much foreigners as they were, but we didn't *look* foreign. And for that reason, we were treated like insiders.

The effect upon my psyche was subtle but tangible. Because I received superior treatment, I *felt* superior. In fact, if I was honest with myself, my emotional self believed I *was* superior. Something deep inside told me that I was treated with greater respect because I deserved it. I belonged in a way that my Turkish neighbors did not, and even though my rational self didn't want it to affect me, that sense of belonging heightened my sense of self-worth. Unfortunately, it also heightened my sense of *us* and *them*.

The groups that define our sense of individual identity—our sense of where we belong—also define that which does not belong. Every human remains profoundly aware of the "other." Jennifer Eberhardt explains that "for nearly fifty years, scientists have been documenting the fact that people are much better at recognizing faces of their own race than faces of other races—a finding dubbed the 'other-race effect.'"[224] This phenomenon is universal, regardless of race or nationality. It also appears very early: "By the time babies are three months old, their brains react more strongly to faces of their own race than to faces of people unlike them."[225]

Scientists believe that repeated exposure leads to a sense of familiarity, which produces trust. Unfortunately, however, humans lump the familiar into one category and the unfamiliar into another. Bias is built in—race shapes the way in which humans see the world. They see one another through the stereotypical lens of "us and them." As journalist Walter Lippmann, the man who coined the term *stereotype*, observed in 1922, "For the most part we do not first see, and then define, we define first and then see."[226]

As social beings, we devote considerable attention to the relational structure of our world. This complex undertaking requires effort. Christina Cleveland points out that the human ability to categorize serves to conserve mental energy:

> We are constantly analyzing situations, trying to predict the behavior of others and attempting to

pinpoint answers to complex philosophical questions. However, this way of living requires a great deal of mental energy, which is tricky because as cognitive misers we don't want to waste mental energy! For this reason, we conserve valuable cognitive resources by categorizing individuals into social groups and relying on information about social group membership to help us interact with an individual and predict his or her behavior.[227]

As noted in the previous section, however, the categories need not be accurate. As long as the story we present to ourselves appears coherent, the categories will suffice.

The mental shortcuts produce bias—"the tendency to favor or dislike a person or thing, especially as a result of a preconceived opinion"[228]—because they draw from preconceptions. Preconceptions especially impact how we perceive the other. Eberhardt offers a telling illustration:

> Simply seeing a black person can automatically bring to mind a host of associations that we have picked up from our society: this person is a good athlete, this person doesn't do well in school, this person is poor, this person dances well, this person lives in a black neighborhood, this person should be feared. The process of making these connections is called bias. It can happen unintentionally. It can happen unconsciously. It can happen effortlessly. And it can happen in a matter of milliseconds. These associations can take hold of us no matter our values, no matter our conscious beliefs, no matter what kind of person we wish to be in the world.[229]

Humans cannot easily regulate their personal bias, even when they are enlightened.

Because of our intuitive inclination to categorize the other, we create ingroups and outgroups. The ingroup provides a strong anchor for personal identity because our sense of self is a social construct. Cleveland notes that humans constantly ask themselves the question "Who am I?" but, she suggests, "the better question might be, 'Who do others think I am?' because our self-concept, the part of our self that holds information pertaining to our identity, is extremely susceptible to outside influences."[230]

The human sense of self-esteem is closely associated with group membership. Because we equate personal identity with group identity, we take specific steps to enhance and guard social status:

> When it comes to group membership, we do four things to maintain positive self-esteem: (1) We tend to gravitate toward and form groups with similar others; (2) once the group is formed we engage in group-serving biases that defend the group's positive identity; (3) we try to increase our status by associating with higher-status groups and distancing ourselves from lower-status groups; and (4) if all else fails we literally disparage other groups because in doing so, we elevate our own group.[231]

One method for increasing self-esteem entails the well-documented phenomenon of "BIRGing" (bask in reflected glory).[232] People develop an increased sense of worthiness when they associate with high-status individuals. The fact that children divide into cliques that denote status is commonly known, but such behavior exists well beyond the playground. Further, absent the opportunity to BIRG, one of the most sure-fire methods to bolster self-esteem comes from putting others down.

Humans quite comfortably make judgments about other people in part because they overestimate how much they know about the outsider. We think of ourselves as complex and nuanced, but the homogeneity effect predisposes us to see the outgroup as flat and two-dimensional. As Malcolm Gladwell quips, "We think we can easily see into the hearts of others based on the flimsiest of clues. We jump at the chance to judge strangers. We would never do that to ourselves, of course. We are nuanced and complex and enigmatic. But the stranger is easy."[233] The ease with which we judge the outgroup helps clarify the pervasive partisan environment of the current American social landscape. Ingroups view outgroups through a stereotypical lens rather than as complex, interesting people, deserving trust and worthy of time and attention. A willingness to "walk a mile in his moccasins" would offer hope for a more nuanced outcome.[234]

12

Factor #2 That Provokes Disunity: Deficiency in the Social Capital of Trust

For human relationships to function cohesively, they require an environment of trust. Trust is social capital—the currency exchanged when we cooperate in groups. Australian journalist Ross Gittins, in an interview with Jonathan Tame, expresses the concept of trust well:

> Trust is believing someone else will act correctly. It enables us to hand our children over to teachers, give our vote to a politician, relax while the pilot flies the plane, put our money in a bank account and share the roads with other motorists. We do these things without anxiety because we believe that the others

involved share our values, will act responsibly and look after our interests ... . With any loss of trust, relational capital diminishes. Society becomes poorer as more time is taken drawing up detailed contracts and regulations, more funds are spent on security, surveillance and policing, and health declines because people grow more anxious.[235]

In other words, trust serves as one of the most valuable commodities in human social functioning. High-trust societies have what Francis Fukuyama calls "spontaneous sociability."[236] With abundant trust, "people are able to organize more quickly, initiate action, and sacrifice for the common good."[237] High levels of trust produce all sorts of economic and social advantages, including lower corruption rates, increased entrepreneurship, and lower economic inequality.

The economic impact of trust became concrete for me a few decades ago when I was visiting the Philippines for the first time. I am always fascinated by cultural differences, and I noted that almost all of the houses were surrounded by eight- to ten-foot walls with glass shards cemented into the cap. Upon closer observance, I was puzzled that several empty lots were similarly walled in. A local informed me that the first thing a builder does when working on a new home is to build a wall. "It's to protect the building materials from theft," he said. "If he didn't build the wall first, the materials would disappear."

That started me thinking about the considerable benefits of living in a high-trust culture. Even in our present day, when shoplifting and other thefts are on the rise, American business still extends a huge reservoir of trust to its customers and non-customers. Think, for example, of the countless number of items that are placed outside the store that would be easy pickings for any passerby with ill intent. Every drop of energy and money that is not expended in the effort to guard one's belongings can be invested in more productive endeavors to build the business.

High trust also results in huge socio-psychological benefits. Current work in neuroscience demonstrates that a person's sense of trust increases the hormone oxytocin:

> When we feel safe and secure, our bloodstream is flooded with oxytocin. This triggers the release of other hormones, specifically serotonin and dopamine, which are some of the most powerful chemicals in our brain … . Serotonin reduces anxiety and improves our mood, and dopamine is associated with positive, goal-directed behaviours that motivate creatures to seek things that are rewarding and keeps us doing those things. It sets in place a virtuous cycle of reinforcement: trust someone → feel good → trust even more.[238]

In short, the pathway to build trust is not complex. To trigger the release of oxytocin in another person, I simply need to engage the other in a trusting way. In turn, the person who feels trusted is less likely to hold back—the circle of trust expands. The feeling of being trusted actually increases one's trustworthiness.[239]

Interestingly, studies demonstrate that our default mode is to believe others tell the truth. Even experts such as prosecuting attorneys, police detectives, and judges have great difficulty detecting when someone lies; they detect the lie only 54 percent of the time on average.[240] Malcolm Gladwell notes,

> We do not behave, in other words, like sober-minded scientists, slowly gathering evidence of the truth or falsity of something before reaching a conclusion. We do the opposite. We start by believing. And we stop believing only when our doubts and misgivings rise to the point where we can no longer explain them away.[241]

Because we believe by default, we become profoundly distressed when we discover others have duped or deceived us.

Trust serves as one of the most valuable commodities in human social functioning.

The United States is currently experiencing a profound downturn in mutual trust. The Pew Research Center has been conducting the National Election Study since 1958, when "about three-quarters of Americans trusted the federal government to do the right thing almost always or most of the time."[242] During the Vietnam War, however, public trust began to decline. It has endured ups and downs through the decades, but since 2007, it has never reached higher than 30 percent:

> Currently, 36% of Democrats and Democratic-leaning independents say they can trust government, compared

with 9% of Republicans and Republican-leaners. Throughout Trump's tenure, more Republicans than Democrats reported trusting the government, though that has flipped since Biden's election.[243]

Social commentator, David Brooks, contends that levels of skepticism have taken on a different, more sinister character, what he calls explosive distrust: "Explosive distrust is not just an absence of trust or a sense of detached alienation—it is an aggressive animosity and an urge to destroy. Explosive distrust is the belief that those who disagree with you are not just wrong but illegitimate."[244] Especially disconcerting, not only has trust of institutions declined in America but so has trust in each other. Historically, in most societies, the level of interpersonal trust remains relatively constant, not so in the United States:

> In America, interpersonal trust is in catastrophic decline. In 2014, according to the General Social Survey conducted by NORC at the University of Chicago, only 30.3 percent of Americans agreed that "most people can be trusted," the lowest number the survey has recorded since it started asking the question in 1972. Today, a majority of Americans say they don't trust other people when they first meet them.[245]

This commentary is especially damning since the United States traditionally identifies as a high-trust society. It indicates a deficit at the core of our nation. Social capital in America, so necessary for the healthy functioning of groups, has severely declined. This results in increasing partisanship, increasing polarization, and a decreasing sense of wellbeing.

13

Factor #3 That Provokes Disunity: Believing That Which Suits Us

"In those days there was no king in Israel.
Everyone did what was right in his own eyes" (Jdg 17:6).

Abandoning the Experts

America's lack of trust manifests itself in a particularly disturbing phenomenon: increasing distrust in expert testimony. As I observed in chapter 7, a major contributing factor to that increase is the way modern readers garner information. The dominating presence of the Internet, along with its offspring, social media, created the opportunity for news seekers to download unfiltered opinions according to their choosing. No longer is information only accessible to the diligent few who brave the subterranean stashes of microfiche in university libraries—one can now do research from the comfort of one's sofa with a mere mouse-click. But to our misfortune, no longer is the information flow filtered by dedicated researchers. Each individual is now bequeathed the responsibility to sort out what is credible—we have become our own experts.

In the "good old days," experts in the news business were recognized by longevity, consistency, and training. The *New York Times*, for example, had an almost universally regarded gravitas because readers, regardless of their political leaning, could point to a decades-long history of reliable reporting. Stories that enlightened the public had been uncovered and documented by trained reporters who had apprenticed under older stalwarts in the trade. Those stories were only brought to press after receiving the go-ahead from senior editors who had also been schooled by long years of experience. The aim was reporting that was both *exhaustive* and *reliable* – thus the NYT motto dating back to 1897: "*All* the News That's *Fit* to Print" (italics mine).

This pattern was not limited to the *New York Times*. In newsrooms across the nation, there was a decided effort to maintain the standard of expertise in reporting. Whether a paper leaned right or left, the public in each community could point to real people on the editorial boards who were trained, not only in information gathering, but in information sorting. They were trained BS detectors. If a story didn't pass the smell test, it wasn't printed. From Portland, Maine to Portland, Oregon, the pattern was repeated in cities and towns across the nation. Trained experts would filter the stories as best they could to provide the public with the most reliable information available. Those who disagreed with the reporting or who wanted to present the information from a different angle were respectfully afforded the venue of letters to the editor.

The Internet effectively removed the editor and substituted it with an algorithm. Now applications like Facebook and YouTube specifically program their search engines to recommend links deemed to be of interest to the reader, inviting them to click one more time (hence the term, "clickbait"). The result, however, is the aforementioned rabbit-hole effect, whereby a viewer is invited to view similar material to that which they already looked at. Confirmation bias is baked into the system. We become our own experts, perhaps, but only in a one-sided perspective. Any opinion that counters that bias, even when that opinion comes from a credentialed authority, is automatically met with distrust.

Distrust of expert testimony has been on full display during the COVID crisis, as multiple directors of public health have had their policy decisions questioned again and again. For example, although Dr. Anthony Fauci experienced a high degree of acceptance from a large percentage of citizens, he was also subjected to extreme and often volatile levels of distrust from others. Despite his outstanding credentials as a recipient of the Presidential Medal of Freedom and over fifty years of service in the public health sector, he has been the target of vitriolic attacks on his character and death threats to his person.

The reality of threats to public officials may have ceased surprising the American public, but the propensity to doubt the word of public officials triggers alarms. As it relates to information about the virus and vaccine efficacy, the locus of distrust is distinctively partisan. For example, in September 2021, 90 percent of Democrats said they had received at least one dose of the vaccine, compared to 58 percent of Republicans.[246] Disturbingly, party affiliation appears to drastically impact the level of trust in broadly sanctioned public health policy.[247]

Another clear instance of distrust in experts has manifested in the controversy over the 2020 election. Former President Trump has been the key promoter of the charge that the election was conducted fraudulently since the election was declared for Biden in November 2020. Consistently close to 75 percent of Republican voters have remained convinced by his arguments. Fully recognizing that I am in misalignment with many of my Assemblies of God tribe, I return to the subject of the "stolen election," this time through the lens of our national loss of trust in experts.

Former President Trump's accusations of election fraud began early and often. He deliberately softened the ground for seeds of mistrust about election integrity, making statements before the 2016 election that "people that have died 10 years ago are still voting" and "voter fraud is very, very common."[248] At a rally in Ambridge, Pennsylvania on October 10, 2016, he urged his supporters to monitor polling places and "watch other communities, because we don't want this election stolen from us."[249]

After winning the election, the accusations continued. Shortly before his inauguration, Trump tweeted that he would "be asking for a major investigation into VOTER FRAUD, including those registered to vote in two states, those who are illegal and … even, those registered to vote who are dead (and many for a long time)."[250] He contended that between three to five million unauthorized immigrants had cast ballots, without which he would have won the popular vote. On May 11, 2017, he appointed Vice President Mike Pence to head a newly formed "Presidential Advisory Commission on Election Integrity." The committee would be abruptly disbanded eight months later without having discovered any evidence of significant fraud. Nevertheless, Trump repeated his claim that massive fraud had taken place and blamed the states for withholding information.

Former President Trump consistently demeaned expert testimony regarding election security and cherry-picked data that could bolster his claims.[251] The constant barrage significantly impacted the electorate's confidence in the system. Sadly, that appears to have been Trump's intent.

Well-schooled in the art of a successful sales pitch, Trump understood that people are readily convinced by an outward show of confidence. Researcher Malcolm Gladwell asserts that humans are not well-equipped to stand up against an assertive person because our default orientation is to believe what someone says. "You believe someone not because you have no doubts about them. Belief is not the absence of doubt. You believe someone because you don't have enough doubts about them."[252]

Because we cannot imagine ourselves pressing and repeating a falsehood that we know has no shred of truth, it is difficult to imagine someone else doing it. We say to ourselves, "It may not all be accurate, but there must be at least some truth to it."

Whether or not former President Trump himself was convinced of the veracity of his arguments will likely be debated for years to come. Through sworn testimony procured by the January Select Committee, we may be certain that multiple members of his inner circle assured him that the charges of widespread election fraud had no basis in fact. I believe we can also safely assert that when Trump chose to continue to propagate the stolen election premise, he well understood how influential his messaging would be.

The former president intentionally took advantage of the human characteristic that the more often people hear an assertion, the more likely they are to believe it is true. As Kahneman observes, "A reliable way to make people believe in falsehoods is frequent repetition, because familiarity is not easily distinguished from truth. Authoritarian institutions and marketers have always known this fact."[253] Because of our preference for cognitive ease, we tend not to be exacting in our deliberations of what may be deceptive unless the discrepancy is flagrant enough to shock us out of System 1 thinking. The more familiar an idea, the more likely we are to assume that it is true. As a skilled marketer, Trump persistently repeated the accusation of widespread election fraud. It was not necessary to prove it or to repeat the whole argument. As

Kahneman discovered in his research, "The familiarity of one phrase in [a] statement sufficed to make the whole statement feel familiar, and therefore true."[254] Simply putting the idea of fraud out there and offering examples of how it *might* take place was enough to convince a large swath of the public that widespread fraud occurred and that Biden's victory was a hoax.

A majority of Republican voters showed a remarkable lack of confidence in public election officials and in court opinions, even courts presided over by Trump appointed judges. Election officials of both parties in the contested states gave consistent testimony that proper procedures had been followed and no significant fraud was evident. After the election, the Trump campaign brought sixty-four lawsuits alleging voter fraud. Nearly all of the suits were very narrow in scope; in only one case concerning the length of time Pennsylvania voters were allowed to fix errors in their mail-in ballots was an injunction granted. The courts found the charges to be indefensible and without merit, often constructed out of whole cloth. To this date, not one instance of fraud that would remotely impact the outcome of any of the 2022 races has been demonstrated.[255]

Where narrow ballot differentials reached the appropriate threshold to call for audits, audits occurred according to prescribed policy. Nevertheless, when Secretary of State Raffensperger declared that the ballot recount in the state of Georgia had been properly conducted and confirmed the Biden win, members of his own party massively challenged his authoritative testimony.[256] Neither his in-group status as a Republican nor his sterling record as a person of exceptional character spared him from vicious ad hominem attacks and even death threats.[257]

Rusty Bowers, the majority leader in the Arizona House of Representatives, became another object of former President Trump's scorn. In testimony given before the January 6th Select Committee, he described how Trump personally telephoned to convince him that he had the authority to convene the legislature, decertify the designated Biden electors for the state of Arizona, and designate an alternative set of electors who would cast their ballot for Trump. His refusal to do so (because it would have been a straightforward breech of his constitutional duty) resulted in a backlash of extreme criticism and threats of violence. MAGA protestors regularly assembled outside his home, blasting over loudspeakers their disapproval, accusing Bowers of being "a pedophile and a pervert and a corrupt politician."[258]

During the hearing, Bowers read an excerpt from his journal in December 2020:

> It is painful to have friends who have been such a help to me turn on me with such rancor. I may in the eyes of men not hold correct opinions or act according to their vision or convictions, but I do not take this current situation in a light manner, a fearful manner, or a vengeful m..anner.
> I do not want to be a winner by cheating. I will not play with laws I swore allegiance to with any contrived desire toward deflection of my deep, foundational

desire to follow God's will, as I believe he led my conscience to embrace.

How else would I ever approach him in the wilderness of life? Knowing that I ask this guidance, only to show myself a coward in defending the course He let me take—He led me to take.[259]

At the time of this writing, it is yet to be seen whether the testimony in the January 6 Select Committee Hearings will result in a significant reset within the Republican Party regarding the charges of election fraud. I am hopeful but not confident. I feel deeply saddened that so many of my fellow Republicans would question the ethical integrity of Rusty Bowers in favor of holding to the version of reality put forth by former President Trump. The insights I have noted throughout this work about the prevalence of cognitive distortions help to explain why.

We must make a distinction between an authority and an authority figure.

I began this section by lamenting the lack of trust in expert testimony. One might argue that former President Trump, with his access to a vast array of intelligence findings, ought to be considered an authority with regard to the election outcome. Shouldn't we afford him more trust rather than less? I believe the answer is no, and I explain that response as follows.

We must make a distinction between an *authority* and an *authority figure*. An authority earns their status through education, apprenticeship, and life-long practice;

an authority figure gains that title via their position, regardless of their actual expertise. Former President Trump is an authority figure who gained that position by campaigning on an *anti-authority* platform. He boasted about *not* being an insider, *not* being a career politician, *not* making his decisions based on institutional knowledge. He appointed many members of his Cabinet because they were outsiders who would shake up the system. The argument was that our country would benefit from policies that defied institutional knowledge. And because Americans have become enamored with the idea that each of us can be our own expert, half the nation was prone to accept the logic.

During his presidency, Trump repeatedly favored his own judgment over the authoritative voices of generals, health officials, and diplomats. During the 2016 election campaign he famously boasted, "I know more about ISIS than the generals do, believe me."[260] After a tour of the CDC headquarters in April 2020, he exclaimed, "People are really surprised I understand this stuff. Every one of these doctors said, 'How do you know so much about this?' Maybe I have a natural ability."[261] After Christopher Krebs, the director of the Cybersecurity and Infrastructure Security Agency, declared that the November election was the most secure in our nation's history, Trump tweeted, "Our 2020 Election, from poorly rated Dominion to a Country FLOODED with unaccounted for Mail-In ballots, was probably our least secure EVER!" Then he fired him.[262]

Former President Trump may be an authority figure, but when it comes to election security, he has no expertise.

On the other hand, Brad Raffensperger, whom Trump disparages, is *the* authority related to the Georgia ballot count. He knows the system intimately, understands how the checks and balances are built in, and has proven his sound judgment through years of faithful public service. The fact that so many voters continue to believe that there was substantial voter fraud in Georgia despite two meticulously executed recounts demonstrates the premise I have repeatedly referenced: when seeking validation for an insider point of view, human beings are profoundly susceptible to cognitive distortions.

I'm reminded of the passage in *The Lion, the Witch and the Wardrobe* in which the children go to the professor, concerned that Lucy, who has been to Narnia and told the others about it, might be going mad.

> "Logic!" said the Professor half to himself. "Why don't they teach logic at these schools? There are only three possibilities. Either your sister is telling lies, or she is mad, or she is telling the truth. You know she doesn't tell lies and it is obvious that she is not mad. For the moment then and unless any further evidence turns up, we must assume that she is telling the truth."[263]

Brad Raffensperger and Rusty Bowers are men of deep faith and deep character—known truth tellers. Both are Republicans. Both actively supported Donald Trump during his candidacy and presidency. Neither has anything to gain by squelching evidence that might support former President Trump's allegations of election fraud. Much the contrary, they suffered severely because they followed their conscience. Thus, like the professor, we ought to reason: We know they don't tell lies and it is obvious that they are not mad (nor are they vindictive). For the moment then and unless any further evidence turns up, it makes the best sense of the situation to assume that they are telling the truth.

The Law of Group Polarization—
Trusting Only My Tribe

Before moving on to consider specific steps we can take to promote unity within the body of Christ, we need to come back to a theme first introduced in chapter 8—something Cass Sunstein in 1997 dubbed "the law of group polarization." To maintain a clear sense of identity, groups tend to emphasize how they differ from other groups rather than their similarities. Sunstein states that the focus on dissimilarity tends to go to extremes: "Group polarization arises when members of a deliberating group move toward a more extreme point in whatever direction is indicated by the members' predeliberation tendency."[264] When given the opportunity to talk with others who share a similar opinion, groups become more cohesive and homogenous. The highs and lows of opinion level out and the graph becomes flatter. In one study that assembled small groups of liberals and separate groups of conservatives to deliberate about a short series of controversial topics, Sunstein noted three characteristic outcomes:

- *More extremism*: "In almost every group, members ended up with more extreme positions after they spoke with one another."[265]

- *Less internal diversity*: The experiment made "both liberal groups and conservative groups significantly more homogeneous—and thus squelched diversity. Before members started to talk, many groups displayed a fair bit of internal disagreement. The group disagreements were reduced as a result of a mere fifteen-minute discussion."[266]

- *Greater rifts*: The discussions served to widen the difference between liberals and conservatives. "Before discussion, some liberal groups were, on some issues, fairly close to some conservative groups. The result of discussion was to divide them far more sharply."[267]

Sunstein attributes the outcomes to three main causes: the transfer of information, the influence of corroboration, and the impulse toward social conformity.

First, what other people do or say informs the observer about what makes sense to do or say. Second, as people express views, others who are unsure of their views will at first feel hesitant to express them. However, as they listen to more views, the unsure person gains confidence in the credibility of what they hear. As they grow in courage to express similar information, the cycle of corroboration gains momentum. Third, and perhaps most importantly, the exchange provides understanding of acceptable attitudes and behaviors within that particular social context. As Sunstein notes,

> Even if people do not believe that what other people do provides information about what should be done, they may think that the actions of others provide information about what other people think should be done. Thus each person's expressive actions come with a *reputational externality*. People care about their reputations, and hence they may do what they think other people *think* they should do, whether or not they believe that they should do it.[268]

The compulsion to conform to the social norms of the group is both powerful and ubiquitous.[269]

David French contends that group polarization profoundly impacts the current American social, political, and religious environment: "The United States is in the grip of a phenomenon called 'negative polarization.' In plain English, this means that a person belongs to their political party not so much because they like their own party but because they hate and fear the other side."[270] People not only disagree with their political opponents, but they also loathe them.

The nation's founders built American democracy upon the notion of healthy pluralism. Alexis de Tocqueville famously observed that

> Americans of all ages, all conditions, and all dispositions constantly form associations. They have not only commercial and industrial companies, in which all take part, but associations of a thousand other kinds—religious, moral, serious, futile, extensive, or restricted, enormous or diminutive.[271]

Tocqueville marveled at the strength and diversity of American associations, which, in his opinion, provide the key to America's economic and social flourishing. The sheer variety and diversity impressed him.

But the landscape has changed: "Healthy pluralism, whereby citizens find meaning in their communities and civic associations secure in the knowledge that the body politic will ultimately protect their autonomy, is in decline. It's being replaced by an increasingly bitter factionalism."[272] Social commentator, Peter Wehner, asserts that the vitriolic nature of the divide between left and right has caused citizens to have utter contempt for the political system: "Many Americans have crossed over a threshold from frustration to despair, from unhappiness to rage, from deep skepticism to corrosive cynicism."[273]

The doctrine of pluralism insists that people with earnestly held, widely differing opinions may live peacefully side by side despite the differences; a democratic government is built upon the possibility of constructive disagreement and compromise. Unfortunately, the willingness to compromise in today's partisan environment has severely diminished.[274] Where no willingness to compromise exsts, deliberative dialogue serves no purpose, and the very foundation of the democratic process erodes.

Many express grave concern that the polarization and unwillingness to compromise are now staple characteristics of American evangelicalism. In an editorial in *Christianity Today* in April 2021, Timothy Dalrymple alerted his readers to the "splintering of the evangelical soul":

New fractures are forming within the American evangelical movement, fractures that do not run along the usual regional, denominational, ethnic, or political lines. Couples, families, friends, and congregations once united in their commitment to Christ are now dividing over seemingly irreconcilable views of the world. In fact, they are not merely dividing but becoming incomprehensible to one another.[275]

Christians are used to divisions due to theological differences or questions about the appropriate response to pressing social issues, but the new fault lines differ—they are deeper, more threatening. They threaten the broadly held conviction within evangelicalism that, despite difference, at least they worked on the same project.

Michael Graham shares the sentiment. He believes that the evangelical church can be best understood as six different camps with wide disparities between the extremes. The polarization in the church reflects the fact that evangelical identity has never been merely theological but social and political:

> The fracturing we are experiencing is likely to be irrevocable as the historical ties that bind have eroded beyond repair. The reality is that while many in the evangelical movement thought their bonds were primarily (or exclusively) theological or missional, many of those bonds were actually political, cultural, and socioeconomic. These political, cultural, and socioeconomic differences have always been there beneath the water line but what has occurred over the last 5-10 years has been the extent to which those values are expressed has been exposed.[276]

When the social and political environment polarizes, so does the Church.

Ryan Burge and Paul Djupe examine the relationship between authoritarian structures in the state and in the church. They state that "without question, the greatest tectonic shift in the recent American religious landscape has been the rise of the Christian Right."[277] The movement "makes religious authority a central feature," and that ideology may have made evangelical churches more responsive to authoritarian political ideology.[278] Concurrently, a distrust of traditional political authorities has been engendered. One study observes, "The passion for order … seems to have led conservative Evangelical leaders to a radical distrust of the very democratic processes they have become adept at using."[279]

The new fault lines differ—they are deeper, more threatening.

One interesting development is the rise in the number of self-described evangelicals during the Trump era, as demonstrated in a September 2021 Pew Research Center survey: "There is solid evidence that White Americans who viewed Trump favorably and did not identify as evangelicals in 2016 were much more likely than White Trump skeptics to begin identifying as born-again or evangelical Protestants by 2020."[280] Some see that as good news. Others point to the possibility that the term *evangelical* has, in the common vernacular, come to refer to moral people with a right-wing political preference.

French contends that when fully 26.7 percent of those who self-identify as evangelical attend church seldom or never (up 10 points from 2008), then the term *evangelical* has changed its meaning.[281] Therefore, unsurprisingly, many theologically conservative evangelicals feel as if a political agenda has hijacked the church they know and love. The question remains: what is the appropriate response? How can the Church pursue unity amid polarization? That is the subject of the next chapter.

14

Pathways toward Genuine Connection:
A Roadmap

"Make every effort to keep the unity of the Spirit through the bond of peace" (Eph 4:3, NIV).

The Church in America suffers under the same polarization that afflicts the broader culture. In an age of extreme partisanship, many seriously question the possibility of a unified community of saints. The Gospel of John informs us that Jesus specifically prayed for unity, and most certainly His prayers align with the will of the Father. Thus, hope for unity remains justified, even during this time when division in the Church pervades. Because the sources of disunity are multifaceted, an adequate response must be multifaceted as well. In this chapter I recommend five key attitudes and actions that foster unity among brothers and sisters who are deeply divided.

Speak to the Elephant

In an age of partisanship, dialogue with one another is difficult. The natural human tendency to speak before listening opposes James's admonition: "Be quick to listen, slow to speak" (Jas 1:19). That sinful tendency exacerbates as partisanship intensifies. Some give up on the hope of constructive dialogue if it involves speaking with a person who holds opposing views, but the pathway of least resistance will not overcome disunity. Yale political science professor Bryan Garsten challenges us to speak directly to one another:

> In addressing our fellow citizens directly, we make an effort to influence them, not with force or threat or cries, but with articulated thoughts that appeal to their distinctly human capacity for judgment. In trying to persuade, we attend to their opinions without leaving behind our own, and so we try somehow to combine ruling and being ruled in the way that democratic politics requires. While neither as powerful nor as ubiquitous as rhetoricians themselves might claim, persuasion is nevertheless a real possibility in democratic life, and it is a possibility that we ought to protect.[282]

Persuasion is both possible and necessary. It consists of more than a mere sales pitch; if we pursue righteousness as the end, persuasion becomes an act of love.

Many have given up on the possibility of persuading others. According to Haidt, the primary motivational motor of human beings is intuition (the elephant), so attempts to address reason directly (the rider) prove mostly ineffectual. He therefore argues that "if you want to change people's minds, you've got to talk to their elephants."[283] At first glance, talking to the elephant seems to run contrary to Garsten's admonition to persuade others "with articulated thoughts that appeal to their distinctly human capacity for judgment."[284] This, however, misses the point of what Haidt asserts. He does not encourage his readers to abandon rational speech; he points out that before the rider can even hear the words, the elephant must lean in.

A person's moral intuition is not set. Socialization, experience, training, and the Spirit of God shape it. If I want to persuade someone morally, it will not suffice for me to confront their ideas. I cannot convince another to adopt a moral conviction by directly confronting their ideas but by coming alongside them.[285] Their intuition will pick up subtle clues—my gestures connoting warmth, eye contact demonstrating attention, my open ears affirming "your thoughts matter to me." Their intuition remains especially attuned to signs of rejection or to misalignment when my words and my attitude do not match. Most essentially, to speak to the intuitive side of someone, I must let them know I am for them.

In an article that has become a missions classic, Donald Larsen introduces an elephant metaphor with a slightly different meaning. Once when Larson was leading a workshop in East Africa, a missionary asked him if he "knew anything about elephants."[286] She went on to explain that when a herd of elephants approaches the water hole that is surrounded by another herd, "the lead elephant of the second group turns around and backs down toward the water hole. As soon as his backside is felt by two of the elephants ... they step aside and make room for him. This is then the signal ... that the first herd is ready to make room for them."[287]

The lesson dovetails wonderfully with Haidt's elephant metaphor. Too often, especially in our exceptionally volatile environment, our approach to the opposition is to come in tusks first. We wield our argument like a sword, ready to slice and dice the opponent's position. But if we are to successfully "speak to the elephant," we must learn to "back in." Tusks first will only instigate tusks back in response.

Dale Carnegie often quoted Henry Ford to illustrate the art of persuasion: "If there is any one secret of success it lies in the ability to get the other person's point of view and see things from their angle as well as your own."[288] It is impossible to persuade another of anything no matter how good the logic if the conversation turns combative. A conversation intent on persuasion must also hold open the possibility of being persuaded. As Haidt observes, "If you do truly see it the other person's way—deeply and intuitively—you might even find your own mind opening in response."[289]

Exemplify Intellectual Humility

Humility is one of the hallmarks of Christian maturity, a trait supremely modeled in Jesus Christ. This essential quality enables one to speak to the elephant. The call to humble oneself, a key component of the journey toward Christlikeness, runs consistently throughout Scripture. Humility indicates personal strength, not degradation. Fundamentally relational, humility regulates one's attitude and behavior toward others.

Everett Worthington describes four characteristics of humility that I find particularly helpful:

> (1) accurate knowledge of one's strengths and weaknesses; (2) teachable spirit regarding all of life, but particularly in non-defensively seeking to acknowledge and correct one's weaknesses; (3) modest self-presentation; and (4) an other-oriented interpersonal style in which one seeks to lift others up even if, at times, this involves letting the other person's interests have precedence.[290]

Notably, these characteristics are fundamentally relational—they show up most clearly in the way we treat others.

I am convinced that humility is more caught than taught. As I pointed out earlier, my father, Dr. Daniel Pecota, provided me with a superb model. A professor at Northwest University for thirty-nine years, he always created a learning culture in which "no question was a dumb question" and in which he not only assumed the role of lecturer but of fellow learner. He was quick with quips such as "The older I get, the more I know what I don't know." Although he was exceptionally disciplined, he was never afraid to share areas of weakness, even with his students.

My relationship with Dad actually thrived under the exceptional challenge that presented itself when I matriculated at Northwest as a freshman and became one of his students. Because he was the primary professor for New Testament Greek and for theology, I attended at least one of his classes in all four years I attended, including all my homiletics and systematic theology courses and a full year of New Testament Greek. After I graduated and began assisting my former youth minister, Bob Stone, in a church plant in Seattle, Bob asked my mom and dad to participate in the fledgling church. My parents readily agreed. That paved the way for me to become my parent's pastor when Bob left to take a pastorate in another city. Within two years I went from being my father's student to being his pastor.

One might assume that my father's relationship to me would remain at least somewhat top-down, but that assumption would be false. One of my father's older colleagues once implied that it must be frustrating or at least a bit boring for Dad to sit under the preaching of his son who had only recently been his student. Dad didn't hesitate: "Quite the contrary! I learn from Steve." Though he was a person of exceptional intelligence, Dad remained intellectually humble. Intellectual humility (IH) "involves taking a humble stance in sharing ideas—especially when one is challenged or when an idea or person presenting the idea is threatening."[291] Insight about the limits of one's knowledge and openness to new ideas are essential elements of IH, along with the ability to regulate one's own arrogance. The challenge to be intellectually humble creates tension for people of faith: "Some religious perspectives equate one's level of religious faith with the amount of certainty that one's religious beliefs are absolutely true, so expressing doubts about the certainty of one's beliefs might be perceived as lacking faith."[292] In other words, when having faith indicates spiritual sincerity and maturity, then expressing doubts or reservations about the content of faith may be understood as a mark of immaturity.

Worthington posits that one must distinguish between religious humility, which "necessarily involves tolerance and open-minded-ness toward alternative religious ideas" and spiritual humility, which embodies an attitude of reverence before God:

> The spiritually humble person, who treats God as most high and other religious objects perceived to be sacred as also holy, sees adherence to religious beliefs, values, and attitudes as a sacred duty. Thus, such a spiritually humble person could not be religiously humble (in the sense of giving up allegiance to sacred beliefs and commitments) without sacrificing his or her spiritual humility.[293]

The distinction remains important, especially in a post-modern cultural atmosphere that treats every truth claim as a power claim. The Christian must respectfully declare that openness to competing religious beliefs is not an option for them.

That does not imply bullheadedness, however. Style has a profound impact:

> In style, the spiritually humble person—humble before God—must still embody the necessary and sufficient

conditions of general humility … . The person could defend religious ideas that he or she endorsed against alternative beliefs, values, and attitudes, if the person did so using a humble style. But if one presents one's dogmatic beliefs in a way that does not value the other person and treats the other person as legitimately and respectably able to arrive at different religious conclusions, then few people would consider the person religiously humble.[294]

This is particularly relevant for Christian leaders. A pastor must never use spiritual certainty as an excuse for disparaging those who disagree. Intellectual humility proves integral to the Christian witness, which leaders ought to practice in all situations, even in the pulpit.[295]

One final element of IH is worth noting: IH entails the capacity to "accurately discern and act upon which beliefs are indeed core and thus almost immutable, which are of moderate importance and thus modifiable upon strong evidence that they should be modified, and which are of low importance and thus are more easily open to contrary evidence."[296] A humble person has the ability to sort the essential from the secondary or subject merely to difference of opinion. In words of the dictum often attributed to St. Augustine: "In essentials, unity; in non-essentials, liberty; in all things, charity."[297]

Choose Civility

P. M. Forni, author of *Choosing Civility*, contends that civility, though in decline in the twenty-first century, "is fundamental to the making of a good, successful and serene life."[298] It involves following rules of conduct that have developed within social structures throughout the world that, in their essence, simply mandate kind and respectful behavior toward one another. For Forni, civility "means practicing the art of giving. This practice is at the same time free and binding. Although not obligatory (not prescribed by law), it creates a bond between those involved."[299]

Peter Wehner describes a hopeful demonstration of civility in the city of Duluth, Minnesota through an organization called the Speak Your Peace Civility Project. They seek to encourage constructive dialogue within their city as a necessary element of the democratic process: "This is not a campaign to end disagreements. It is a campaign to improve public discourse by simply reminding ourselves of the very basic principles of respect."[300] The organization adopted nine rules from Forni's book as guidelines for productive dialogue.[301] Mayor of Duluth, Emily Larsen, credits the civility project with helping the city negotiate an emotionally charged debate over an ordinance requiring paid sick leave. Larsen believes that "truly listening" helps people discover that they have common ground, which in turn "lays the groundwork for the next conversation."[302]

Truly listening, a key component of civil discourse, requires considerable discipline. We tend to focus on our own arguments or the proposed rebuttal of the other's arguments before actually listening to what the other has to say. Instead, one ought to set the bar high in evaluating one's personal listening style. Daniel Dennett suggests a set of rules developed by the social psychologist and game theorist Anatol Rapoport as guidelines for self-evaluation:

1. You should attempt to re-express your target's position so clearly, vividly, and fairly that your target says, "Thanks, I wish I'd thought of putting it that way."

2. You should list any points of agreement (especially if they are not matters of general or widespread agreement).

3. You should mention anything you have learned from your target.

4. Only then are you permitted to say so much as a word of rebuttal or criticism.[303]

Dr. Jim Heugel, provost of Northwest University, provided me with an excellent model of Rapoport's first point. A few years ago, I invited him to teach a seminar on Islam in our adult education program. Before Jim started the course, he declared to us that it was his intent to present the information in such a manner that if a Muslim attended the course, they would respond with, "That's a very fair assessment of what we believe." That impressed me as an appropriate goal whenever we attempt to describe the beliefs of people who disagree with us. After the meeting, Keith, one of our congregants, informed me that as Jim made the statement, he was seated next to a professed Muslim who had come in response to our post on the Internet. When Keith spoke with him at the close of the meeting, it was apparent that our guest was roundly impressed with Jim's knowledge of the topic but most especially with his open-hearted approach.

To improve the character of constructive disagreement in and around their congregations, spiritual leaders must strive to demonstrate Rapaport's level of respect toward the views of all challengers, whether in the pulpit, in leadership settings, or in conversations with outsiders. Though a tall order, it is not impossible; such an attitude precisely corresponds to Christ's model of humility and kindness.

Broaden the Circle

Perhaps the most important step believers can take to promote unity in the body of Christ is to broaden their personal circle of relationships. Social psychology demonstrates that we respond much more positively to the ideas and opinions of other people if we have a relationship with them. Simply developing personal friendships can break down biased attitudes toward the other, yet in most congregations, circles of association remain persistently homogenous. This is particularly true of their racial makeup.[304]

Bridging Racial Barriers

The racial divide has proven to be a persistent challenge to the experience of unity in the body of Christ. The famous words of Martin Luther King, Jr. unfortunately still ring as true today as in 1960: "I think it is one of the tragedies of our nation, one of the shameful tragedies, that eleven o'clock on Sunday morning is one of the most segregated hours, if not the most segregated hour in Christian America."[305] Nevertheless, hopeful efforts toward integration continue. Kevin Dougherty observes, "More Americans are attending religious services with others who do not look like them … . The increase is slow but steady, and there is no sign that we've reached a plateau."[306] But Dougherty warns that increased diversity does not result in greater racial justice. The mere presence of multiple races within a congregation does not make multiethnic friendships more likely. The influence of the homophily principle (the tendency to choose groups that reflect one's own social and demographic background) remains persistent.[307]

In 1954 Gordon Allport posed the contact hypothesis, which asserts that prejudice toward groups that are different may be reduced or eliminated if the two parties have positive contact with each other.[308] Multiple studies have largely supported his hypothesis, albeit only when the contact fulfils certain conditions:

> The key conditions under which interaction is theorized to lead to positive change include groups enjoying equal status, cooperative contact between groups, development of shared goals, and a supportive authority structure … . [Researchers have since] added a fifth condition to the model: opportunity for the development of cross-group friendships. [309]

The set of conditions has important implications for Christ followers, for they present a picture of how the Church ought to function—equal status, cooperative contact, shared goals, and a supportive authority structure, all bound together in genuine multiethnic friendships. These reflect the characteristics of unity that Jesus enjoyed with His Father: a shared identity, a shared purpose, and a shared perspective.

Christian leaders have a responsibility to encourage cross-group friendships within their congregations. The best vehicle for doing so is to model the behavior by building cross-group friendships themselves. As Cleveland notes,

> To be a follower of Christ means to care deeply about and pursue other followers of Christ, including the ones that we don't instinctively value or like. We need to adopt the belief that to be a follower of Christ means to allow our identity as members of the body of Christ to trump all other identities. We need to adopt the belief that to be a follower of Christ means to put our commitment to the body of Christ above our own identity and self-esteem needs.[310]

Pastors can and should take the first steps in this direction.

My own journey in building interracial friendships has been one of fits and starts. Having grown up in Kirkland (yes, the birthplace of Costco), I was not exactly surrounded by people of color. While writing this, I couldn't remember any Black students in my high school, so I pulled out my senior yearbook to check. My memory was correct, sort of. There was not a single Black student in my graduating class and only three Black underclassmen who I had never met. I also confirmed a very small number of Asian and Latino students.

Our church was also a nearly color-free zone. When a Black family with eight children moved into the Roosevelt District and were invited by the neighborhood Sunday School bus captain to start attending, they were probably just as surprised to be there as we were to see them. Douglas, the youngest brother, told me recently that the day at junior high summer camp when I, as a counselor, invited him to spend a couple hours sailing together, was a significant memory for him. It meant something to him that a college senior was genuinely interested in who he was and what made him tick. As you might imagine, his affirmation is how I'd like to think of myself. But that is only part of the story.

My most embarrassing racial moment is painful to share, but I include it because it reveals the blinders under which I labored. We didn't often have people of color visit Calvary Chapel, the church I helped to plant and pastored for a decade. One Sunday morning, a Black university student visited for the first time, invited by a fellow classmate. I was thrilled to see him and, as was our custom, asked him along with the other visitors that day to briefly introduce themselves. When his turn came, he smiled broadly and said, "Hi, my name is Kin."

At least that's what it sounded like to me, but I wasn't quite sure. To explain the setting, our church leased space from a Seventh Day Adventist congregation—a beautiful gothic structure with an abundance of stained glass and a very high, vaulted ceiling. The acoustics worked wonderfully for the congregation to hear the pastor, but they worked terribly in reverse.

I said to the young man, "I'm sorry, I didn't quite get that." So, he repeated, "I'm Kin."

Now I was getting embarrassed. It still didn't sound right. "I'm sorry, it's hard to hear up here. Did you say Kim?"

"No! I'm Ken" It still sounded like Kin. "K-E-N!"

Now I was utterly embarrassed. But unfortunately, I did not remain speechless. Out of the desire to somehow explain myself, I uttered the fateful line: "Oh, Ken! You say it, Kin … we say it Ken."

Needless to say, 200 sets of eyes shot daggers my way, training their shock and disgust and embarrassment on their pastor for what he had just said. I felt horrible. Our normal liturgy was to take a little break to greet one another at that point, so I immediately sought out the young man and apologized. He was gracious to me and took it in stride. To no surprise, however, he never did come back.

Looking back nearly forty years, it's difficult to believe I could have been that socially inept and unaware of my own words. But over the years I have learned that the attempt to justify oneself often blinds us to the bigger picture. That incident also revealed an issue of the heart. My use of "you" and "we" (so obvious to me now, but so imperceptible to me then) unveiled that the caring, accepting, diversity affirming pastor I wanted to be was not who I in fact was.

A huge part of my deficit in relating to people of color is that I don't know their stories. When working with staff and board members of color, I often took the color-blind approach—in effect trying to act as if race didn't matter. After all, "The ground is level at the foot of the cross," I said to myself. But in trying to ignore race, it was too easy to miss differences of perspective and areas of heightened sensitivity. So, when a new Black staff member responded to my first words of correction in a decidedly defensive manner, it was at first hard for me to perceive where that was coming from. I tried to treat him as an equal but failed to see that there were at least two levels of separation between us—my authority as a senior pastor *and* my race.

I was also oblivious to why a Black committee member (a very successful business executive), responded with such agitation when I allowed another member of the committee to criticize his ideas in a meeting. In my mind, it was a fair give and take among peers. I assumed that since he had achieved such a level of success, he had nothing to prove. From his perspective, having worked so hard throughout his life to overcome barrier after barrier, my decision not to immediately cut short the criticism from a junior member was an unacceptable failure of leadership. I might have foreseen his response had I taken more time in advance to learn his story.

The more I hear stories from friends of color, the more I empathize with their experiences. During the protests relating to the murder of George Floyd, a Black woman of Caribbean origin in our small group told us of her sense of dread because her two sons were driving through Montana and Idaho on their way from their university on the East Coast back to Seattle. She was terrified what might happen if they were pulled over. Her fear came as a surprise to me— it's something that would never cross my mind concerning my own children. But of course, that's exactly the point.

During The Unity Project, a participating pastor of Filipino descent shared about an encounter in a church she and her husband used to serve in. One Sunday, a person she considered to be a close friend called her by the name of another Filipino woman in the congregation. When she pointed out the error, her friend said without apology, "Oh, I just can't keep you people apart. You all look alike!" Her friend never even recognized how hurtful those words were.[311]

Another participant offered a helpful perspective on the Black Lives Matter movement. He stated that although the organization itself has some dubious elements that are decidedly contrary to the gospel, the heart of the message ought to be heeded. He pointed out that the insistence of many of his White friends that "all lives matter" is more than mildly insensitive. "Imagine," he told us, "that you have a daughter who is dying of cancer, and you share it with a friend and that friend replies, 'Lots of children get cancer.' That is how it comes across to many Black people when they hear the phrase, 'all lives matter.'" His metaphor helps me relate to his feelings on a visceral level.

> Rather, broadening my circle means that my own identity expands. I come to see myself as a part of a family that is vastly more expansive and more heterogeneous than I had imagined.

The quest to broaden the circle is essentially an effort to increase the database we rely upon when considering an issue or making a judgment. The greater the number of stories we have to fall back on, the greater our capacity for empathy. It does not mean abandoning my own culture and my own catalogue of experiences. Rather, broadening my circle means that my own identity expands. I come to see myself as a part of a family that is vastly more expansive and more heterogeneous than I had imagined.

Adopting my identity in Christ does not mean that I relinquish my own cultural identity. Cleveland observes that to ignore one's culture "would violate the metaphor of the body of Christ, in which each group expresses its unique perspective and function in coordination with other groups and in submission to the head, Jesus Christ."[312] Colorblindness is not the prescribed pathway, for color comes from God's multifaceted gift to His people. Rather, as believers discover their identity within the multiethnic family of God, they can appreciate and celebrate the Father's wonderfully diverse color pallet.[313]

Bridging Political Barriers

Politics is another arena in which we must intentionally broaden the circle. Though difficult, it is not impossible for those with opposing political views to speak with one another in a civil, open, and ultimately productive manner. It is not unusual to hear older members of Congress wistfully reminisce about the days when cross-party friendships were the norm, concluding that it is no longer possible in today's polarized environment. But examples persist of politically active people who have pushed past the temptation to villainize the other side and have built genuine connection with their political opposition.

Sarah Stewart Holland and Beth Silvers are two sorority sisters who have successfully labored to bridge the divide. In their book, *I Think You're Wrong (But I'm Listening),* Sarah, a Democrat, and Beth, a Republican, tell how they began dialoguing with each other and eventually started a podcast called *Pantsuit Politics.* Their conviction is that "having calm, kind conversations from opposing perspectives is more than possible—it is a spiritual imperative."[314]

Holland and Silver admit that conventional wisdom dictates that we avoid the subjects of politics and religion; however, that is not what we actually do. We do not avoid talking about politics altogether; we avoid talking about politics with those who disagree with us:

> We changed "you shouldn't talk about politics" to "you should talk only to people who reinforce your worldview." Instead of giving ourselves the opportunity to be molded and informed and tested by others' opinions, we allowed our opinions and our hearts to harden.[315]

We thus miss out on a key building block in our own emotional and intellectual maturity—having our views challenged.

As long as we tie our identity to the positions we hold, we are much more likely to absolutize that position. But if our first order identity is "I am a child of God," then we are likely to allow room for nuance. We are also more likely to genuinely love those whose political convictions differ from our own. There is considerable room for differences of opinion, even among those who are deeply committed to Christian orthodoxy. As Holland and Silver observe:

> You can believe in gun control and care about the Second Amendment. You can acknowledge the existence of man-made climate change and God ... You can be against drug use and pro-legalization. You can pray every night and believe prayer in school is problematic.[316]

As much as believers care about moral standards over which government has influence, they must also acknowledge that Christian orthodoxy is not tied to any one political party.

Holland and Silver suggest a simple, two-part pattern for overcoming the political barrier: looking inward and looking outward. Looking inward involves the willingness to acknowledge "a hard spiritual truth we all learn over and over as people of faith: any problem, political or otherwise, starts with us. Blaming or, worse, trying to control others is never the solution."[317] The observant reader will recognize that the identical theme runs throughout this book. Only by clothing ourselves with humility (1 Peter 5:5) will we be able to appropriately repent for the ways in which we have contributed to the division.

Then we are prepared for step two: turning our eyes outward in order to reconnect as brothers and sisters. The goal is not absolute agreement on every principle, but to prioritize relationships over differences. "We are bringing the principles we value in our faith and our lives—understanding, curiosity, and, above all, grace—to our civic engagement."[318] The essential element is that we stay in conversation with one another rather than cutting off the communication.

Two institutions in Virginia, Georgetown University and a small conservative Christian institution, Patrick Henry College, have initiated a very creative tool for reaching across the political and social divide. They call it *In Your Shoes*. A professor from each school challenged their theater students to team up with a partner from the other school. They asked the participants to do a deep dive into their partner's world view and experiences. Then they took their partner's own words and feelings, turned them into a script, and dramatically performed that script before a live audience. Derek Goldman, head of Georgetown's Performing Arts Department and one of the innovators of the project, says that his students "feel like they're in these kinds of bubbles with people who agree with them and feel the same way they do, and then they're at odds with a whole set of other people."[319] The aim of the project is to break the students out of those bubbles and to force them to empathetically interact with someone whose views differ radically from their own.

Does it work? Two of the participants who were partnered with each other shared their impressions in a live interview:

> *Myiah Smith*: You talk all the time to people. I mean, we have TikTok and Instagram. We can record videos and listen back to it. But very rarely do people share word for word the things that you have shared … What's different is now I have had

the opportunity to practice and grapple and build language and habit to appropriately converse with those people.

Interviewer: Mikey, what was it like for you to say Myiah's words?

Michael "Mikey" Pozo: It was beautiful. Being able to capture someone's words, and it coming from your own mouth, you can really say, this is what she says, this is what he believes in, and I'm going to repeat it to her... The person who is a liberal, I can still take care, I can still have love for. And I cherish that person.[320]

In Your Shoes forces the students to truly listen to someone different than themselves. Unsurprisingly, that results in a level of understanding and empathy that never would have occurred through the stereotypical interchange between liberal and conservative.

Choose to Embrace

One of the inevitable consequences of hurtful speech, exclusionary practices, and prideful partisanship within the Church is that relationships will be damaged. Miroslav Volf, who endured the brutal ethnic conflict of Bosnian war, writes profoundly about the real possibility of reconciliation, even when relationships appear irreparably broken. His experience is apropos for this moment in the American Church.

Volf points to the literal and metaphorical expression of "the embrace" as a way forward. He observes that in the drama of embrace, there are four acts. Act one is opening the arms. In opening my arms, we reach out for the other. Open arms "are a sign of discontent with your own self-enclosed identity, a code of *desire* for the other."[321] I think of how my children, when they were small, instinctively opened their arms to me in an expression of longing for connection, affirmation, and comfort. In opening our arms, we take the initiative—we begin the process by creating a space into which the other can enter.

Act two is *waiting*. "The open arms reach out but stop before touching the other. They wait."[322] The open arms signal willingness, but don't force the situation. They are a sign that the full autonomy of the other is respected.

Act three is *closing* the arms. This is the goal—the hoped for result—and it requires reciprocity. Volf says, "It takes two pairs of arms for one embrace … . In an embrace a host is a guest and a guest is a host."[323] Volf also notes that "a soft touch is necessary."[324] This is not a bear-hug, nor is it a complete surrender in a "self-destructive act of abnegation."[325] Balance is called for. We maintain personal boundaries yet open ourselves to the other at the same time. And we must recognize that simply opening oneself to the other does not necessarily mean that we understand them. In fact, we must cultivate "the unusual ability *not* to understand the other."[326]

Act four is *opening* the arms again. "What holds the bodies together in an embrace is not their welded boundary, but the arms placed around the other. And if the embrace is not to cancel itself, the arms must open again."[327] The two do not become one—the embrace does not erase differences. Rather, the fact that they embraced changes each of them just a little bit. Here we see a key in human interaction that pursues unity. It is not about changing the other but pursuing a connection; and if the connection is genuine, change will be the natural result.

For some who are not natural huggers, Volf's encouragement to embrace feels more like a threat than an invitation. I believe Volf's language allows us the space to embrace the metaphor, even if we resist a physical hug. Nevertheless, physical touch remains one of the most important ways for humans to connect with each other. It is exceedingly unfortunate that one of the side effects of the COVID-19 crisis is a lingering reluctance to embrace that many people experience. At first, that reluctance was truly necessary in order to guard against infection and to some extent that remains true. But COVID-19 is a sad reminder that in our fallen world, multiple enemies will always be at work to prevent human beings from connecting with one another as God designed them to do.

After admonishing his readers to pursue the ritual of embrace, Volf crafts a final fitting metaphor for how humans benefit by pursuing connections to those who differ from us:

> There are always strangers within our personal and communal gates and we ourselves never belong completely to a given group but only in part. As individuals and communities, we live in overlapping social territories. Ourselves and our communities are like our domiciles in which we feel at home, and yet keep remodeling and rearranging, taking old

things out and bringing new things in, often objects acquired on visits to near and distant places, objects which symbolize that we can never be the same after we have ventured out of our home, that things we encounter "outside" become a part of "inside."[328]

That metaphor resonates deeply with me. As missionaries and lifelong travelers, my wife and I are well aware of the deep delight that results when we are able to incorporate some custom or object of value from another culture into our own. Some of our favorite traditions are those we garnered through our years of residence in Germany. As Volf observes, "we live in overlapping social territories" and from that mixture we derive our greatest joys.

To promote unity within our congregations, Christ followers must become avid souvenir collectors. We must intentionally search out the objects of value that are to be found among those who are quite different than us, adding to our own framework the treasures we acquire through visits with other travelers, both near and distant.

Concluding with Three Central Implications

The doctoral project that ultimately spawned this book was birthed during the post-election period in late 2020. It seemed as if I was watching the Church splinter before my very eyes, and I wanted to figure out why. What factors impact our moral judgments? Why do our partisan loyalties blind us? How do cognitive distortions hinder our ability to judge correctly? Most importantly, what can we do to heal the divisions in today's Church?

The Unity Project that was central to my doctoral work provided a practical workshop for promoting unity in the Church—a living illustration of how spiritual leaders with differing opinions can move toward the oneness Jesus prayed for. After researching intently, overseeing The Unity Project, and writing this book, I remain convicted of three central implications.

- **Unity Deserves the Highest Level of Attention by Spiritual Leaders.** The Unity Project calls renewed attention to Christ's prayer that believers might be one "so that the world may believe that you sent me" (John 17:21). Unfortunately, the Church often wavers in its commitment to behavior that promotes the fulfillment of that prayer. The research in this book demonstrates that cognitive biases, which all humans manifest with regularity, provoke disunity and partisan thinking. To resist that tendency, spiritual leaders must model intellectual humility before their congregations. By making every effort to embody humility and bestow trust on others, they provoke those in their spiritual care to do the same, thus building a foundation for unity. The phrase "make every effort" (Eph 4:3) ought to remind us that a passion for unity entails strenuous activity. In other words, it does not spontaneously happen— we must work at it!

- **Unity Remains Exceedingly Difficult to Maintain**. Unfortunately, partisanship in contemporary American culture pushes its way into the Church. Unity has multiple enemies. This study demonstrates that stubborn loyalty to our in-group, from which we draw our sense of identity, provokes seeing "the other" as a threat, even when "the other" may be a brother or sister. The groups we belong to both bind and blind us. To overcome the blindness, spiritual leaders must take deliberate action.

One powerful enemy of unity includes the sinful tendency to capitulate. Regarding race one might argue: "Segregation is simply a fact of human nature. The important thing is that the Gospel is preached." Or regarding politics: "People get cranky over politics. That's just the way it is and it's not going to change. Better to leave that topic out of the church." Unfortunately, spiritual leaders often succumb to the false conviction that, because the gospel is not political and transcends racial labels, it's better to steer clear of race and politics. But it is precisely topics like race and politics in which the darkness of the human heart is most clearly revealed and where "hatred, rivalry, jealously, outbursts of anger, quarrels, conflicts, factions" (Gal 5:21) most come to the fore. God calls spiritual leaders to confront all the deeds of the flesh, including those that manifest in our most polarizing issues. In this book I have argued that a church is healthier when it consists of members who differ from one another on issues such as race, politics, and social justice. Therefore, spiritual leaders must continually point the way toward nuanced dialogue that seeks first to understand before seeking to be understood. Fulfilling that calling will always remain difficult.

- **Unity Requires Cooperating with the Holy Spirit and with One Another.** "It seemed good to the Holy Spirit and to us," wrote the apostles to the church in Antioch (Acts 15:28). Genuine unity springs out of spiritual soil, cultivated by listening carefully to what God says and to what our brothers and sisters say. Such careful listening requires discipline and desire. Unity among believers need not remain a distant, unachievable goal, but it will remain out of reach unless believers make room for both the Holy Spirit and their fellow Christians in their hearts, which necessarily implies pushing out other objects that tend to crowd the heart—namely pride, self-serving behavior, and the right to be right.

When I first read *The Gulag Archipelago* in college, the words of Aleksandr Solzhenitsyn left a lifelong impact upon my thinking: "Pride grows in the human heart like lard on a pig."[329] The tendency for self-exaltation remains hard baked into the human spirit and only overcome through the influence of God's Spirit upon our own.

It is perhaps an oversimplification (but perhaps not) that the problem of disunity in the Church is a pride problem. In any case, unity cannot prevail apart from the willingness to "in humility count others more significant than yourselves" (Phil 2:3).

I sincerely pray ...

that spiritual leaders will exemplify that attitude in heart, mind, and action;

that they will teach it to their congregations;

that their congregations may reveal a renewed spirit of unity to their communities; and

that the world may know that the Father sent the Son.

Glossary

Availability Heuristic—A method of making judgments based upon the information that is immediately available to the mind. Availability is often connected with the cognitive distortion WYSIATI: "What you see is all there is."[330]

Confirmation Bias—"The tendency to selectively search for or interpret information in a way that that confirms one's preconcept-ions or hypotheses."[331]

Halo Effect— The tendency to take one data point and extrapolate it to the whole, even though the data points may be unrelated. For example: "She speaks well; she must be a good leader."

Heuristic—A rule of thumb or mental shortcut that the mind uses to make a judgment or decision. Technically, a heuristic is "a simple procedure that helps find adequate, though often imperfect, answers to difficult questions."[332]

In-Group Bias—"The tendency for people to give preferential treatment to others they perceive to be members of their own group."[333]

Partisanship—"Strong and sometimes blind adherence to a particular party, faction, cause, or person."[334] Robust group loyalty tends to bind members to one another and blind them to alternative views.[335]

Racism—"A learned dogma in which one ethnic person or group claims or assumes superiority over another."[336] Racism is "generally characterized by hostility, contempt or condescension, and readily leads to social, economic and political mistreatment of others."[337]

Representativeness Heuristic—A method of making judgments based upon a preconceived notion or prototype. People tend to judge two things as similar if they meet the criterion of the prototype, even though the similarities may be quite limited.

Systemic Racism—Also known as institutional or structural racism, the term describes a form of racism that is embedded through laws into a society or organization.

Tolerance— "Sympathy or indulgence for beliefs or practices differing from or conflicting with one's own."[338] In this work the term refers to the willingness to humbly treat all human beings with dignity and respect.

About the Author

Steve Pecota is a pastor with over forty-five years of experience in student ministry, church planting, and marriage enrichment. Alongside his mentor, Bob Stone, Steve co-founded Calvary Chapel, Seattle in 1975, a church that focused on students at the University of Washington. He and his wife, Karen, subsequently enjoyed nearly two decades living in Hamburg, where they ministered with Students for Christ, helped begin Marriage Encounter in German speaking Europe, and planted Christliche Gemeinde Norderstedt.

Steve and Karen returned to the U.S. in 2007 to pastor the church in which he grew up. There they experienced the unique joys and challenges of pastoring a traditional church with a long, vibrant history.

Steve has degrees from Northwest University (B.A.), Fuller Seminary (M.A.), and Assemblies of God Theological Seminary (D.Min.). Early in 2022, he completed his doctoral project on the subject: "Promoting Unity in the Body of Christ in an Age of Extreme Partisanship."

Steve and Karen reside in Seattle, Washington, where they presently care for Karen's aging mother. They have two grown married children, Kevin (& Amy) and Kathryn (& John). Steve and Karen take great joy in following God's path, wherever it leads.

Endnotes

Foreword

1   Martin Luther King, *Stride toward Freedom: The Montgomery Story* (Boston: Beacon Press, 1958, 1986), quoted in John Dear, "The God at Dr. King's Kitchen Table," January 16, 2007, National Catholic Reporter, accessed November 4, 2022, https://www.ncronline.org/blogs/road-peace/god-dr-kings-kitchen-table.

2   N. T. Wright, *After You Believe: Why Christian Character Matters* (New York: HarperOne, 2012), 106, quoted in Peter Amsterdam, "Jesus—His Life and Message: The Sermon on the Mount," Director's Corner, August 4, 2015, accessed November 4, 2022, https://directors.tfionline.com/post/jesushis-life-and-message-sermon-mount-introductio/.

3   James M. Kouzes and Barry Z. Posner, *The Leadership Challenge*, 4th ed. (San Francisco: Jossey-Bass, 2007).

4   Jeff Brumley, "Outgoing SBC President Affirms Conservative Values while Decrying Legalism," Baptist News Global, June 15, 2021, accessed November 4, 2022, https://baptistnews.com/article/outgoing-sbc-president-affirms-conservative-values-while-decrying-legalism/#.Y2TAKuzMLxo.

5   Ryan Foley, "Al Mohler Suggests Christians Who 'Vote Wrongly' Are 'Unfaithful': 'The Big Battles Are Still to Come," The Christian Post, September 19, 2022, accessed November 4, 2022, https://www.christianpost.com/news/al-mohler-christians-vote-right-way-midterms.html.

6   Morgan Marietta and David C. Barker, *One Nation, Two Realities: Dueling Facts in American Democracy* (New York: Oxford University Press, 2019).

7   Eugene H. Peterson, *A Long Obedience in the Same Direction: Discipleship in an Instant Society* (Downers Grove, IL: InterVarsity Press, 2021.

8   N. T. Wright, "Why Unity is the Church's Greatest Calling," N. T. Wright Online, July 22, 2022, accessed November 4, 2022, https://www.youtube.com/watch?v=qn7KdqCx1No.

Introduction

9   Francis A. Schaeffer, *The Mark of the Christian* (Downers Grove, IL: InterVarsity Press, 1970), 27.

10   All Scripture quotations, unless otherwise indicated, are from the English Standard Version.

11   Olivia Eubanks, "'Unprecedented' Named People's Choice 2020 Word of the Year by Dictionary.com," ABC News, December 16, 2020, accessed October 21, 2021, https://abcnews.go.com/Politics/unprecedented-named-peoples-choice-2020-word-year-dictionary/story?id=74735664.

12   David Brooks contends that Americans have reached a new level of distrust that he calls explosive distrust: "Explosive distrust is not just an absence of trust or a sense of detached alienation—it is an aggressive animosity and an urge to destroy. Explosive distrust is the belief that those who disagree with you are not just wrong but illegitimate." David Brooks, "America Is Having a Moral Convulsion," *The Atlantic*, last modified October 5, 2020, accessed September 25, 2021, https://www.theatlantic.com/ideas/archive/2020/10/collapsing-levels-trust-are-devastating-america/616581/.

See Emily Ekins, "Poll: 62% of Americans Say They Have Political Views They're Afraid to Share," Cato Institute, last modified July 22, 2020, accessed August 26, 2021, https://www.cato.org/survey-reports/poll-62-americans-say-they-have-political-views-theyre-afraid-share; See also Matthew H. Graham, "Democracy in America? Partisanship, Polarization, and the Robustness of Support for Democracy in the United States," *The American Political Science Review* 114, no. 2 (May 2020): 392–409.

13   Michael Graham, "The Six Way Fracturing of Evangelicalism," *Mere Orthodoxy*, last modified June 7, 2021, accessed June 22, 2021, https://mereorthodoxy.com/six-way-fracturing-evangelicalism/.

14   Timothy Dalrymple, "The Splintering of the Evangelical Soul," *Christianity Today*, accessed June 22, 2021, https://www.christianitytoday.com/ct/2021/april-web-only/splintering-of-evangelical-soul.html.

15   Schaeffer, *The Mark of the Christian*, 26.

16   Ibid., 31-35.

17   See Matthew D. Lieberman, *Social: Why Our Brains Are Wired to Connect* (New York: Crown Publishers, 2013).

18   They observe, "Democracies work best—and survive longer—where constitutions are reinforced by unwritten democratic norms. Two basic norms have preserved America's checks and balances in ways we have come to take for granted: mutual toleration, or the understanding that competing parties accept one another as legitimate rivals, and forbearance, or the idea that politicians should exercise restraint in deploying their institutional prerogatives." Steven Levitsky and Daniel Ziblatt, *How Democracies Die* (New York: Crown Publishing, 2018), 8.

19   Kahneman acknowledges that it is extremely difficult to overcome the power of cognitive distortions. For example, he quips, "Can overconfident optimism be overcome by training? I am not optimistic." Daniel Kahneman, *Thinking, Fast and Slow* (New York: Farrar, Straus and Giroux, 2010), 264. The general tenor of his work indicates that the more people understand how their minds work, the better equipped they are to avoid both obvious and obscure pitfalls.

Chapter 1: Created for Community—The *Imago Dei*

20   All Scripture quotations, unless otherwise noted, are from the English Standard Version.

21   Stanley Grenz, *Renewing the Center: Evangelical Theology in a Post-Theological Era* (Grand Rapids, MI: Baker Books, 2006), 213.

22   Karl Barth, *The Doctrine of Creation, Part 2*, vol. 3 of *Church Dogmatics* (Peabody, MA: Hendrickson Publishers, 1960), 48-49. Other theologians have also adopted the theme of community as a central, integrative motif for theology. Stanley Grenz is a powerful voice for this direction. Grenz observes that the emphasis on individualism that has been predominant in Western thought is waning in the face of the growing understanding in the social sciences that our sense of identity is tightly tied to the community around us. He argues, "Community is crucial to identity formation. Our sense of personal identity develops through the telling of a personal narrative, which, communalists declare, is always embedded in the story of the communities in which we live." Stanley J. Grenz, *Theology for the Community of God* (Grand Rapids, MI: Wm. B. Eerdmans Publishing Co, 2000), 48.

23   Barth, *The Doctrine of Creation, Part 2*, 247. Barth observes, "'I am'—the true and filled 'I am'—may thus be paraphrased: 'I am in encounter.' ... At the very root of my being and from the very first I am in encounter with the being of the Thou, under his claim and with my own being constituting a claim upon him. And the humanity of human being is this total determination as being in encounter with the being of the Thou, as being with the fellow-man, as fellow-humanity. To this extent we must oppose humanity without the fellow-man." Ibid.

24   Barth, *The Doctrine of Creation, Part 2*, 250. He observes, "The human significance of the eye is that we see one another eye to eye. It is man who is seen in this way, not things, or the cosmos ... . It is man who is visible to man, and therefore as the other, as the one who is thus distinct from the one who sees him." Ibid.

25   Ibid.

26   Ibid., 252. Barth states, "It is a good thing to see and be seen. But there is a good deal more to humanity than that ... . On the plane of mere seeing, the one who sees has to form his own picture of the other, understanding the man himself and what he is and does from his own standpoint, and measuring and judging him by his own standards." Ibid., 252-253.

27   M. Scott Peck, *The Road Less Travelled: A New Psychology of Love, Traditional Values and Spiritual Growth* (New York: Touchstone, 1978), 127.

28   Stephen R. Covey, *The 7 Habits of Highly Effective People: Restoring the Character Ethic* (New York: Simon & Schuster, 1989), 239.

29   Barth, *The Doctrine of Creation, Part 2*, 260.

30   Ibid.

31   Ibid.

32   Ibid., 265.

33   I once participated in an anointing service in which the pastor poured oil from a vessel directly over the participants' heads. I can attest that the gentle trickle of oil running down the head and through the beard and then further down over the shoulders is quite intoxicating, especially as the body heat warms the oil as it descends. David, the author of this psalm, no doubt related this experience to his own anointing to the kingship of Israel.

34   Leslie C. Allen, *Psalms 101-150*, Word Biblical Commentary 21, rev. ed. (Nashville: Thomas Nelson, 2002), 279.

35   D. A. Carson, *Christ & Culture Revisited* (Grand Rapids, MI: Eerdmans Publishing Co., 2008), 46.

36 David French, "How Systems Kill," accessed August 25, 2022, https://frenchpress.thedispatch.com/p/how-systems-kill.

37 Ibid., 49.

38 When God rejected Cain's offering, Cain felt excluded from God's favor and this sense of rejection went to the core of his identity. His reaction was to carry out the ultimate exclusionary act and to murder his brother. But God was not excluding Cain; he was instead delineating for him the nature of their relationship. It included boundaries which were essential because of God's otherness. Miroslav Volf notes, "The absence of boundaries creates nonorder, and nonorder is not the end of exclusion but the end of life." Miroslav Volf, *Exclusion and Embrace: A Theological Exploration of Identity, Otherness, and Reconciliation* (Nashville: Abingdon Press, 1996), 63. God desired to embrace Cain, but not on Cain's terms that essentially denied God's right to determine the boundaries. Cain, in this account, bears a theological similarity to the older brother in Christ's parable of the prodigal. Both desired embrace but on their own terms.

Chapter 2: Jesus and the New Community

39 The Puritan fathers demonstrate a particularly lucid recognition of how pride stands in the way of spiritual maturity, hence the necessity of being self-aware. Thomas Watson (1620-86) writes, "A humble man values others at a higher rate than himself, and the reason is he can see his own heart better than he can see another's. He sees his own corruption and thinks surly it is not so with others; their graces are not so weak as his; their corruptions are not so strong. 'Surely,' he thinks, 'they have better hearts than I.' A humble Christian studies his own infirmities and another's excellences and that makes him put a higher value upon others than himself. 'Surely I am more brutish than any man' (Prov 30:2)." Thomas Watson, *The Godly Man's Picture* (Edinburgh: Banner of Truth Trust, 1992), 79.

40 Andrew T. Lincoln, *Ephesians*, Word Biblical Commentary 42 (Waco: Word, 1990), 235.

41 Leon Morris, *The Gospel According to John*, rev. ed, (Grand Rapids, MI: Eerdmans, 1995), 551.

42 Commentators differ concerning the timing of the so-called Upper Room Discourse after the meal concluded. The end of John 14 assumes an immediate departure, but then the discourse continues for two more chapters. "An old view is that the departure did not take place as the end of chapter 14 and that the following chapters are words spoken as the little group walked to Gethsemane. This is not impossible, but cannot be proven." Morris, *The Gospel According to John*, 559. Whether the discourse beginning in 13:31 took place in the Upper Room as the meal drew to a conclusion or while it was underway or both, which seems to me most likely, these words of our Lord obviously left a vivid impact in the mind of Apostle John and are among the most precious that are recorded.

43   George R. Beasley-Murray, *John*, Word Biblical Commentary 36, 2nd ed. (Nashville: Nelson, 1999), 247.

44   Francis A Schaeffer, *The Mark of the Christian* (Downers Grove, IL: InterVarsity Press, 1970), 22.

45   Schaeffer offers a helpful complement to this observation: "If I fail in my love toward Christians, it does not prove I am not a Christian. What Jesus is saying, however, is that if I do not have the love I should have toward all other Christians, the world has the right to make the judgment that I am not a Christian." Ibid., 24.

46   Ibid., 27.

47   Morris, *The Gospel According to John*, 649.

48   Schaeffer, *The Mark of the Christian*, 31.

49   Ibid., 30.

50   Richard B. Hays, *Echoes of Scripture in the Gospels* (Waco, TX: Baylor University Press, 2016), 342. John makes use of two metaphors that inform Jesus's prayer for oneness: "The branches that abide in the Vine and the one flock gathered from among the nations to follow the One Good Shepherd. The power of these images is derived from their grounding in the earlier scriptural portrayals of God's desire to unify and heal the nation of Israel through one future just and benevolent king. The Evangelist John, however, draws upon these images to reimagine the church's position in the world. John is transforming and expanding these biblical images. Through these transformations, John's Gospel echoes the voice of the divine Shepherd who seeks to lead his people beyond a gloomy picture of the church huddled fearfully together, and into a grace-filled life offered to the whole world." Ibid., 343.

51   David R. Maxwell, "The Nicene Creed in the Church," *Concordia Journal* 41, no. 1 (2015): 15.

52   Morris observes that some very good manuscripts read "God the only begotten" (μονογενὴς θεὸς) and this reading "seems to have both better attestation and transcriptional probability on its side." Morris, *The Gospel According to John*, 100. "Only begotten God" sounds strange to our ears, but it punctuates the continuing union of the Son with the Father that is affirmed in the next phrase which is best translated "he who is in the bosom of the Father" (ὁ ὢν εἰς τὸν κόλπον τοῦ πατρὸς). Ibid., 101.

53 Joel C. Elowsky, ed., *John 1-10*, vol. IVa of *Ancient Christian Commentary on Scripture* (Downers Grove, IL: InterVarsity Press, 2006), 54.

54 Ibid.

55 Morris, *The Gospel According to John*, 101.

56 Morris notes that Jesus's declaration "is an emphatic form of speech and one that would not normally be employed in ordinary speaking. Thus to use it was recognizably to adopt the divine style." Ibid., 420.

57 Christena Cleveland, *Disunity in Christ: Uncovering the Hidden Forces That Keep Us Apart* (Downers Grove, IL: InterVarsity Press, 2013), 82.

58 Elowsky, *John 1-10*, 191.

59 Chrysostom confirms the point: "But why didn't he say that 'he does nothing contrary' instead of 'he cannot do'? It was so that he might again show the invariableness and exactness of the equality, for the expression does not impute weakness to him. On the contrary, it shows his great power." Ibid., 190.

60 Barth, *The Doctrine of Creation*, Part 2, 250.

Chapter 3: Unity on What Basis?—The Jerusalem Council

61 F. F. Bruce points to the importance of the moment: "The Council of Jerusalem is an event to which Luke attaches the highest importance; it is as epoch-making, in his eyes, as the conversion of Paul or the preaching of the gospel to Cornelius and his household." F. F. Bruce, *The Book of Acts*, rev. ed. (Grand Rapids, MI: Eerdmans Publishers, 1988), 282.

62 N. T. Wright, *Paul: A Biography* (New York: HarperOne, 2018), 134-135.

63 Paula Fredriksen argues that the Early Christian movement was firmly rooted in the soil of Judaism but that the close connection is often lost on modern readers, in part because of the incendiary language Paul used to describe his apostolic colleagues who differed with him regarding the nature of Gentile participation in the church. In Fredriksen's view, Luke's account of the Jerusalem Council, written several decades after it took place, deliberately softens the intensity of the conflict: "The calm council that Luke depicts in Act 15 represents a narrative form of wishful thinking." Paula Fredriksen, *When Christians Were Jews: The First Generation* (New Haven, CT: Yale University Press, 2018), 157. J. Lyle Story disagrees: "These terms reflect Luke's portrait of the early Christian communities from sources that he trusts; perhaps these descriptions, which might seem to us now as idyllic and idealized, also appeared to Luke as reasonably consistent with what he was currently observing." J. Lyle Story, "Luke's Instructive Dynamics for Resolving Conflicts: The Jerusalem Council," *Journal of Biblical and Pneumatological Research* 3 (2011): 104.

64   Wright, *Paul*, 135.

65   Ibid., 140.

66   In Pauline chronology, one of the biggest issues relates to whether Galatians 2:1-10 is understood as Paul's description of the events of the Jerusalem Council. Pierson Parker represents the most prevalent view: "It certainly looks as though these accounts cover the same history, for it would be hard to imagine two such councils, on the same subject, involving the same people, with the same sequence of events, in the same places, and with the same denouements—right down to a quarrel between Paul and Barnabas." Pierson Parker, "Once More, Acts and Galatians," *Journal of Biblical Literature* 86, no. 2 (June 1967): 176. F. F. Bruce concurs: "The great majority hold that Luke and Paul report the same occasion." F. F. Bruce, *The Book of Acts*, rev. ed. (Grand Rapids, MI: Eerdmans Publishers, 1988), 283. If that is the case, the confrontation of Peter at Antioch necessarily followed the council. Others contend that the Antioch controversy preceded the council and therefore informs our understanding of what was at issue during the council. For example, Cornelis Bennema argues: "The majority view holds that Gal 2:1-10 relates to Acts 15 and that, therefore, the Antioch crisis occurred after the Jerusalem council … . Contra the majority view, I seek to support Richard Bauckham's proposal that the Antioch crisis was the lead-up to the Jerusalem Council and that the Jerusalem church remained central by providing authoritative direction for the entire Christian mission." Cornelis Bennema, "The Ethnic Conflict in Early Christianity: An Appraisal of Bauckham's Proposal on the Antioch Crisis and the Jerusalem Council," *Journal of the Evangelical Theological Society* 56, no. 4 (December 2013): 753-54.

67   In eating with Gentiles, Peter had been behaving very much like his master, who was willing to break multiple social norms in order to enjoy table fellowship with all manner of saints and sinners. Craig L. Blomberg notes, "When we turn to the synoptic Gospels, we discover Jesus challenging the purity laws of his day, or at least the way in which they are applied to exclude various categories of Israelites. Scandalously, he associated with the notoriously wicked, but he is willing to eat with the scrupulous religious leaders as well. Jesus' table-fellowship with sinners reflects his willingness to associate with them at an intimate level, but not merely for the sake of defying convention or enjoying a party. In each case various textual clues, if not explicit statements, demonstrate that Christ is indeed calling them to repentance and summoning them to become his followers." Craig L. Blomberg, *Contagious Holiness: Jesus' Meals with Sinners* (Downers Grove, IL: InterVarsity Press, 2005), 167. Seen from that perspective, Peter's pulling back from eating with Gentile Christians was a serious departure from the example Jesus had set.

68   Wright, *Paul*, 145.

69   Story detects an eight-point pattern for conflict resolution in Acts 15. They are (1) Acknowledge the divine initiative; (2) celebrate the inclusionary and saving-activity of God; (3) be committed to unity; (4) value the "stories" of others; (5) discern the activity of the Holy Spirit; (6) find direction in the Scriptures; (7) be sensitive to the need for compromise in making decisions; and (8) practice clear communication of decisions. Story, "Luke's Instructive Dynamics for Resolving Conflicts," 99-118.

70   Bruce, *The Book of Acts*, 290.

71   Ibid.

72   Varma states, "So, considering the close proximity (apparently) of Paul's chastising of Peter for introducing distance from Gentile Christians on the basis of a conception of purity, one could not be blamed for being surprised that Peter did take a stand in Acts 15. Nevertheless, a stand he took, and a courageous one at that. In the face of the same detractors that he faced in Antioch, at the Council Peter passionately engages not only the issue at hand—whether Gentiles Christians should be circumcised—but also the theological rationale for the Pharisees' claims. Peter boldly goes where faithful old covenant Jews would never dare go before: he dismisses the claim of purity of himself and fellow Jews, both past and present, on account of failed faithfulness. In its place, he posits the same grace of Christ and the same Spirit of Christ for Jews and Gentiles alike." Ashish Varma, "Jews and Gentiles Together in Christ? The Jerusalem Council on Racial Reconciliation," *Ex auditu* 33 (2017): 172-173.

73   Varma, "Jews and Gentiles Together in Christ?" 173.

74   Ibid., 172.

75   Timothy Gervais sheds light on this thought: "The NRSV translation of the words leading up to James' citation of Amos may be somewhat misleading. The NRSV reads: 'This agrees with the words of the prophets, as it is written.' However, the phrase in the Greek: 'καὶ τούτῳ συμφωνοῦσιν οἱ λόγοι τῶν προφητῶν, καθὼς᾽ γέγραπται,' reverses the order of correlation, making a more appropriate translation 'the words of the prophets agree with this thing.' This difference is significant for Luke's argument, as it deliberately asserts that the cited scripture from Amos should be interpreted in light of God's dealings with the Gentiles, not the other way around." Timothy Gervais, "Acts 15 and Luke's Rejection of Pro-Circumcision Christianity," *Journal of Theta Alpha Kappa* 41, no. 2 (Fall 2017): 12.

76   "The Hebrew text says nothing about Gentile inclusion in the people of God but affirms that God will restore David's fallen tent, 'so that they may possess the remnant of Edom and all the nations that bear my name.' However, the LXX suggests the inclusion of other people and nations, so that 'the remnant of men may seek the Lord.' The LXX translates 'they may possess' (יירש) with 'they may seek' (ידרשו) and 'Edom' (אדם) with 'men' (מאדו). The similarity of sounds of the two pairs no doubt caused the confusion of translation with an addition or transposition of a Hebrew radical. Thus, the LXX text affirms the missionary message of the OT with the inclusion of the Gentiles." Story, "Luke's Instructive Dynamics for Resolving Conflicts," 112.

77   Joseph A. Fitzmyer, *The Acts of the Apostles: A New Translation with Introduction and Commentary* (New York: Doubleday: 1997), 557.

78   The only outlier is the prohibition against πορνεία (fornication). The readiest explanation for its inclusion is that in the holiness code of Leviticus 17-18, the prohibitions against eating blood and against various unlawful sexual relations are listed side by side. James's choice of these four standards reflects how central the holiness code was to the Jewish church. It is noteworthy that Leviticus 17:10 specifically states that the prohibition against eating blood applies to any alien living among them: "If any one of the house of Israel or of the strangers who sojourn among them eats any blood, I will set my face against that person who eats blood and will cut him off from among his people" (Lev 17:10). For Jewish Christ-followers, it made sense that these prohibitions, in particular, carried a moral weight beyond the purity codes related to kosher eating. Bennema takes a somewhat different tach, arguing that the prohibitions were not merely an accommodation to the sensitivities of the Pharisaic believers: "James's ruling was not about compromise, whether couched as cultural sensitivity, pragmatism, or accommodating conservative views. It was … about a concrete scriptural argument to guide the entire Christian mission." Bennema, "The Ethnic Conflict in Early Christianity," 761.

79   Story, "Luke's Instructive Dynamics for Resolving Conflicts," 104.

80   Bruce asserts that the decision was accepted by Peter, who was "the bridge-builder among the apostles" and likely recommended it to the churches in the course of his missionary journeys: "As for Paul, he took a different line. Where true religion and basic Christian ethics were involved, he was as peremptory as anyone could well be in directing his converts to avoid idolatry and fornication. But in matters (like food) which were religiously and ethically neutral, he refused to lay down the law. No food, he maintained, was 'common or unclean' per se—not even if it had been forbidden by the law of Moses, not even if it came from an animal that had been sacrificed to a pagan divinity." Bruce, *The Book of Acts*, 285.

Chapter 4: Unity in the Ministry of Paul

81   "Now the works of the flesh are evident: sexual immorality, impurity, sensuality, idolatry, sorcery, *enmity, strife, jealousy, fits of anger, rivalries, dissensions, divisions, envy*, drunkenness, orgies, and things like these" (Gal 5:19-21, italics mine).

82   There is no indication later in the letter that the teachers who are named (Cephas, Apollos) participated in the quarreling, as noted by Johannes Munck, *Paul and the Salvation of Mankind* (Atlanta, GA: John Knox Press, 1959), 157.

83   Gordon Fee notes that there were at least four issues involved in the conflict, which have implications for the contemporary Church also impacted by partisan spirit. First, "there is 'quarreling' and 'divisiveness' among them, with their various teachers as rallying points." Second, "this quarreling is in some way being carried on in the name of wisdom." The term wisdom "dominates the discussion in chaps. 1-3." *Sophia* is mostly used by Paul in a pejorative sense, indicating that the Corinthians were fond of the term, but not Paul.

Third, there is repeated reference to boasting by the members of the church, particularly boasting about certain leaders. Fee says, "The whole response has a decidedly apologetic ring to it, in which Paul is defending not only his past ministry among them, but also his present relationship to them." Members are apparently puffed up for the teachers they have accepted as heroes and puffed up against Paul (4:6) But Paul understands that this attitude will ultimately prevent them from accepting the needed correction that he is trying to bring. Gordon Fee, *The First Epistle to the Corinthians* (Grand Rapids, MI: Eerdmans Publishing Company, 1987), 47-49. Fee contends that the Corinthians had perhaps been led "to think of their new-found faith as an expression of Sophia—the divine Sophia, to be sure, but Sophia nonetheless. With this kind of context, they were quarreling over their leaders as teachers of wisdom, boasting in one or the other, and judging them from this merely human perspective. From this perspective, neither Paul nor his gospel comes off very well. The message of a crucified Messiah, preached by an apostle who lived in considerable weakness, is hardly designed to impress the "wise," as they now considered themselves." Fee, *The First Epistle to the Corinthians*, 49.

84 Anthony C. Thiselton, *The First Epistle to the Corinthians*, The New International Greek Testament Commentary (Grand Rapids, MI: Eerdmans, 2000), 145. Thiselton further observes, "If everything rests on human cleverness, sophistication, or achievement, the cross of Christ no longer functions as that which subverts and cuts across all human distinctions of race, class, gender, and status to make room for the divine alone as sheer unconditional gift." Ibid.

85 Fee, *The First Epistle to the Corinthians*, 68.

86 Pauline authorship of Ephesians is widely disputed in contemporary scholarship. Andrew Lincoln declares that "the more I have worked on the text as a whole, the more persuaded I have become that seeing the letter as the work of a later follower of Paul makes better sense of its contents" and that "this is now the consensus view in NT scholarship, though a sizeable minority continues to uphold Pauline authorship." Andrew T. Lincoln, *Ephesians*, Word Biblical Commentary 42 (Waco: Word, 1990), lx, lxii. I am convinced by the minority and agree with Markus Barth: "Certainly the doubts regarding authenticity of Ephesians are honest expression of the theological assumptions fostered by some interpreters, and as such they are most revealing. But so far, they have revealed more of the interpreters' minds than of a convincing alternative to Pauline authorship." Markus Barth, *Ephesians: Introduction, Translation and Commentary on Chapters*

1-3 (Garden City, NY: Doubleday & Company: 1974), 49. Against the argument that Ephesians represents a personality lacking in the fire of Paul's temperament, Barth's observation remains poignant: "Though Paul was capable of writing or dictating letter in boiling wrath, with cynical irony, or in the midst of streaming tears, his occasional outburst of temperament did not oblige him to explode all the time. It may be wishful thinking, but it is by no means impossible that—just as it is true of good wine—the old one is milder." Barth, *Ephesians*, 50.

87 Markus Barth, *Ephesians: Translation and Commentary on Chapters 4-6* (Garden City, NY: Doubleday & Company: 1974), 428.

88 Lincoln, *Ephesians*, 143. The new creation here is corporate, not individual. Paul wants none of our Western individualism that limits redemption to a personal decision for Christ. It is so much more than that. As Lincoln observes, "Here Christ, particularly through his death … is seen as the creator of a new humanity." Ibid.

89 D. Martyn Lloyd-Jones, *Christian Unity: An Exposition of Ephesians 4:1-10* (Grand Rapids, MI: Baker Books, 1980), 41.

90 Curtis Heffelfinger, *The Peace Making Church: 8 Biblical Keys to Resolve Conflict and Preserve Unity* (Grand Rapids, MI: Baker Books, 2018), 23.

91 Timothy S. Lane and Paul David Tripp, *How People Change* (Greensboro, NC: New Growth Press, 2006), 79.

92 Barth, *Ephesians 4-6*, 428

93 Dietrich Bonhoeffer, *Life Together* (London: SCM Press Ltd, 1954), 18.

94 The Greek for *cunning* is κυβεία and literally means the throw of the dice. "In the ancient world dice-playing frequently had negative connotations of trickery, and the player was thought of as a wily and cunning customer." Lincoln, *Ephesians*, 258. The Greek for scheming here is μεθοδεία and is used only one other time in the NT—in 6:11 in relationship to Satan's schemes.

95 Barth states that αληθεύω may sometimes be translated as "to cherish," "to maintain," "to live the truth," but that meaning cannot be applied here. As in Galatians 4:16, Paul uses the word in the narrow sense of "saying the truth" or preaching the gospel. Barth, *Ephesians 4-6*, 444.

96 In contemporary preaching, the challenge to "speak the truth in love" is most often interpreted as an encouragement to speak hard truths to one another. See David Augsburger, *Caring Enough to Confront* (Grand Rapids, MI: Revel, 2009), 15. While interpreters ought not to render this text as an encouragement to loving confrontation, the admonition to bring correction to fellow sojourners "in a spirit of gentleness" (Gal 6:1-2) is clearly supported in other passages.

97 Verse 13, Gk. *εἰς ἄνδρα τέλειον*, KJV "unto a perfect man." "*τέλειος* has the nuance of mature rather than perfect, while *ἀνήρ* denotes here an adult male, a full-grown man. The emphasis is on the mature adulthood of this person in contrast with the children mentioned in the next verse." Lincoln, *Ephesians*, 256.

98 Fee, *The First Epistle to the Corinthians*, 666.

99 As Fee observes, "In Paul's view what make the Corinthians one is not just their common article of faith, but especially their common experience of the Spirit, the very Sprit responsible for and manifested in the great diversity just set before them (vv. 4-11)." Ibid., 668.

100 Fee notes that "there is considerable difference of opinion as to what experience(s) this language refers to." Fee, *The First Epistle to the Corinthians,* 604. Multiple commentators contend that Paul is here referring to baptism in water that Christians practice as a symbol of initiation into the faith. For example, Fitzmyer states that "Even though he adds the mention of the Spirit, it is highly unlikely that Paul is referring to anything different than the well-known early Christian tradition about baptism by water and its effects." Joseph A. Fitzmyer, *The Acts of the Apostles: A New Translation with Introduction and Commentary* (New York: Doubleday: 1997), 477. In that case, "baptized in one Spirit" and "given one Spirit to drink" are parallel phrases that both refer to the initiation into the body of Christ that is represented in the baptismal rite. Fee contends that most likely "Paul is referring to their common experience of conversion and does so in terms of its most crucial ingredient, the receiving of the Spirit." Fee, *The First Epistle to the Corinthians*, 671.

101 Fee, *The First Epistle to the Corinthians*, 672.

Part 2 Two Historical Case Studies

102 Andy Crouch, *Culture Making: Recovering Our Creative Calling* (Downers Grove, IL: InterVarsity Press, 2009), 97-98.

Chapter 5: The Community of Pre-Constantine Christians

103 The full quote reads: "'Look,' they say, 'how they [Christians] love one another' (for they themselves hate one another); 'and how they are ready to die for each other' (for they themselves are readier to kill each other)." Tertullian, *Apologeticus* ch. 39, sect. 7.

104   Religions revitalize by "effectively mobilizing people to attempt collective actions." Rodney Stark, *The Rise of Christianity: A Sociologist Reconsiders History* (Princeton, NJ: Princeton University Press, 1996), 78.

105   Andy Crouch, *Culture Making: Recovering Our Creative Calling* (Downers Grove, IL:

InterVarsity Press, 2009), 156.

106   Ibid., 156.

107   Dionysius, "Festival Letters," Book 7, 22, in *Eusebius, The Church History*, trans. Paul L. Maier (Grand Rapids, MI: Kregel Publications, 2007), 240-241.

108   Stark, *The Rise of Christianity*, 89.

109   Crouch, *Culture Making*, 157.

110   H. Richard Niebuhr, *Christ and Culture* (New York: Harper and Row, 1951).

111   Joe Perticone, "How 'Owning the Libs' Became the Ethos of the Right," *Business Insider*, accessed July 19, 2022, https://www.businessinsider.com/how-owning-the-libs-became-the-ethos-of-the-right-2018-7.

Chapter 6: Unity as a Characteristic of Pentecostal Revival

112   William W. Menzies, *Anointed to Serve* (Springfield, MO: Gospel Publishing House, 1971), 9.

113   "To borrow from sociologist Ann Swidler, Pentecostal theology is much more like a mixed tool kit of ideas than it is a tightly-reasoned doctrinal system." Douglas G. Jacobsen, *Thinking in the Spirit: Theologies of the Early Pentecostal Movement* (Bloomington, IN: Indiana University Press, 2003), x.

114   These words are attributed to Joseph Smale, the Spurgeon College educated pastor from England who led the First Baptist Church in Los Angeles and, in 1905, came into contact with the Welsh Revival during a holiday in England. Cecil M. Robeck Jr., *Azusa Street Mission and Revival: The Birth of the Global Pentecostal Movement* (Nashville: Nelson Reference & Electronic, 2006), 58-60.

115   "Asa Mahan's *The Baptism of the Holy Ghost* (1870) and Reuben A. Torrey's *The Baptism with the Holy Spirit* (1895) demonstrate that the question of this baptism was already posed by those in the Holiness movement." Oliverio, *Theological Hermeneutics*, 9-10.

116   Edith Blumhofer, *The Assemblies of God: A Chapter in the Story of American Pentecostalism*, vol. 1 to 1941 (Springfield, MO: Gospel Publishing House, 1989), 85.

117   "Seymour had a vaguely unsettling effect on others—an effect enhanced by the blindness of one eye." Robert Mapes Anderson, *Vison of the Disinherited: The Making of American Pentecostalism* (New York: Oxford University Press, 1979), 60.

118   Gaston Espinosa, *William J. Seymour and the Origins of Global Pentecostalism: A Biography and Documentary History* (Durham, NC: Duke University Press, 2016), 50.

119   Espinosa, *William J. Seymour*, 55.

120   Robeck, *Azusa Street Mission*, 6

121   Ibid., 9.

122   Ibid., 10.

123   Ibid.

124   Ibid., 13.

125   Harvey Cox in his forward to Espinosa, *William J. Seymour*, xvi. Dale Irvin confirms the theological importance of the interracial relationships, as he refers to a November 1906 issue of *The Apostolic Faith*: "The pages of the Azusa Street mission's own paper had already indicated the importance of this experience late in 1906: 'It is noticeable how free all nationalities feel. If a Mexican or German cannot speak English, he gets up and speaks in his own tongue and feels quite at home for the Spirit interprets through the face and people say Amen. No instrument that God can use is rejected on account of color or dress or lack of education. This is why God has so built up the work.'" Irvin continues, citing an *Apostolic Faith* article from January 1907: "An edition published two months later made its theological meaning even more explicit: [God] 'recognizes no flesh, no color, no names … . Azusa Mission stands for the unity of God's people everywhere. God is uniting His people, baptizing them by one Spirit in one body.'" Dale T. Irvin, "'Drawing All Together in One Bond of Love': The Ecumenical Vision of William J Seymour and the Azusa Street Revival," *Journal of Pentecostal Theology* 3, no. 6 (1995): 27.

126   Espinosa observes that allowing Seymour to participate at any level was a violation of the Jim Crow segregation laws. Espinosa, *William J. Seymour*, 50.

127   Charles Parham, *The Everlasting Gospel* (Baxter Springs, KS: Apostolic Faith Church, 1911), 72-73.

128   Oliverio, *Theological Hermeneutics*, 8

129   Frank Bartleman, *How Pentecost Came to Los Angeles*, n.p., n.p., 1925, Academia, accessed August 11, 2021. https://www.academia.edu/6982309/How_Pentecost_Came_to_ Los_Angeles_Frank_Bartleman, 54

130   Cox, *Fire from Heaven*, 58.

131   Ibid., 58.

132   See James R. Goff, Jr., *Fields White unto Harvest: Charles F. Parham and the Missionary Origins of Pentecostalism* (Fayetteville, AR: The University of Arkansas Press, 1988), 11.

133   Espinosa, *William J. Seymour*, 128.

134   William J. Seymour, *The Doctrines and Disciplines of the Azusa Street Apostolic Faith Mission of Los Angeles, Cal.* (Los Angeles: Apostolic Faith Mission, 1915), 13.

135   Cecil Robeck notes, "Seymour's compromise which limited white participation in mission business and which urged blacks to follow the Bible must be viewed, then, not as a final solution to the racial problem, but as an interim solution 'for peace,' a concession to human frailty upheld by an increasingly segregationist racism which was permeating American society, including the church. It was a pragmatic expediency which Bishop Seymour hoped would provide all of his flock 'greater liberty and freedom in the Holy Spirit.'" Cecil M. Robeck, "The Past: Historical Roots of Racial Unity and Division in American Pentecostalism," *Cyberjournal for Pentecostal-Charismatic Research* (2005): 27-28.

136   Renea Brathwaite observes that each of these individuals had "at least three things in common: they were all white; they all tried to usurp Seymour s control over some aspect of the mission; and they all spoke in tongues." Renea Brathwaite, "Tongues and Ethics: William J. Seymour and the 'Bible Evidence': A Response to Cecil M. Robeck, Jr." *Pneuma* 32, no. 2 (2010): 218.

137   Espinosa, *William J. Seymour*, 105.

138   Renea Brathwaite sums up Seymour's practical and

theological reasoning for the shift of emphasis: "If indeed these people [Parham, Lum, and Durham] were baptized in the Spirit, how is it that they behaved in such a fleshy and unethical manner? Seymour's response was to qualify carefully his position on the evidentiary value of tongues. First, he insisted that tongues-speech did not automatically qualify a person for ministry. Second, he affirmed that no one should be considered to have Spirit baptism on the basis of tongues alone. Third, he inveighed against the idea that speaking in tongues was equivalent to Spirit baptism. Fourth, he rejected the notion that tongues were essential for salvation and in-dwelling of the Holy Spirit. Fifth, he argued that tongues were neither an indication of doctrinal purity, nor a substitute for Christian character." Renea Brathwaite, "Tongues and Ethics: William J. Seymour and the 'Bible Evidence': A Response to Cecil M. Robeck, Jr." *Pneuma* 32, no. 2 (2010): 218-219.

139   J. R. Flower, *The Pentecost*, Nov/Dec. 1910, 9.

140   *The Apostolic Faith*, 1.3, November 1906, 2.

141   *The Apostolic Faith* 1.4, December 1906, 2.

142   Dale Irvin, "'Drawing All Together in One Bond of Love': The Ecumenical Vision of William J. Seymour and the Azusa Street Revival," *Journal of Pentecostal Theology* 3, no. 6 (1995): 40.

143   For example, "The interpretation of many of the messages in nearly every language spoken by the Holy Ghost in unknown tongues is that Jesus is coming." *The Apostolic Faith* 1.8, May 1907, 3.

144   Irvin, "'Drawing All Together in One Bond of Love,'" 45.

145   Blumhofer, *The Assemblies of God*, 195.

146   Robeck, *The Past*, 31.

147   Ibid., 32.

148   *The Apostolic Faith*, 1:3, November 1906, 1.

149   I am reminded of the Phillips Translation of Romans 12:2, which states, "Don't let the world around you squeeze you into its own mould."

Chapter 7: Human Brains Are Hardwired for Relationships

150   Matthew D. Lieberman, *Social: Why Our Brains Are Wired to Connect* (New York: Crown Publishers, 2013), 18.

151   Ibid., 19.

152   Ibid. Lieberman attributes this fine tuning to the evolutionary process. A theist directs thanks heavenward and marvels at the grace of the triune God who created humankind in the image of His social self.

153   Ibid., 42.

154   Ibid., 51-59.

155   Ibid., 59.

Chapter 8: First Metaphor—System 1 and System 2

156   Daniel Kahneman, *Thinking, Fast and Slow* (New York: Farrar, Straus and Giroux, 2010), 43.

157   Michael Lewis, *The Undoing Project: A Friendship That Changed Our Minds* (New York: W. W. Norton & Company, 2017), 153.

158   Cass R. Sunstein and Richard Thaler, "The Two Friends Who Changed How We Think about How We Think," *The New Yorker*, December 7, 2016, accessed September 8, 2021, http://www. newyorker.com/books/page-turner/the-two-friends-who-changed-how-we-think-about-how-we-think.

159   Ibid.

160   Christena Cleveland, *Disunity in Christ: Uncovering the Hidden Forces That Keep Us Apart* (Downers Grove, IL: InterVarsity Press, 2013), 44.

161   Kahneman, *Thinking, Fast and Slow*, 21.

162   Ibid., 21-22.

163   Ibid., 20.

164   Ibid., 90. Kahneman goes on to say, "We are endowed with an ability to evaluate, in a single glance at a stranger's face, two potentially crucial facts about that person: how dominant (and therefore potentially threatening) he is, and how trustworthy he is, whether his intentions are more likely to be friendly or hostile." Ibid.

165   Ibid., 65.

166   If your answers were 10 cents, 100 minutes, and 24 days, then you are among the majority. System 1 simply "knew" the answers and came to the logical conclusion. Except that the conclusion in this case was neither logical nor correct. The correct answers are 5 cents, 5 minutes, and 47 days. Those who came to the proper conclusion were exercising System 2.

167   Ibid., 119.

168   Ibid.

169   Ibid.

170   Ibid., 122.

171   Ibid., 97.

172   Lewis, *The Undoing Project*, 183.

173   Jennifer Eberhardt, *Biased: Uncovering the Hidden Prejudice That Shapes What We See, Think, and Do* (New York: Penguin Books, 2020), 61.

174   Ibid., 62.

175   Representativeness plays a role in death penalty decisions. One study measured how the physical characteristics of defendants impacted the likelihood of them being sentenced to death for the crime of murder. Eberhardt notes, "Of the men rated low in stereotypical features, only 24 percent were sentenced to death. But more than 57 percent of the 'highly stereotypical' black defendants were sentenced to die for their crimes. Looking 'more black' more than doubled their chances of being sentenced to death, even though we controlled for factors like the severity of the crime, aggravating circumstances, mitigating circumstances, the defendant's socioeconomic class, and the defendant's perceived attractiveness." Eberhardt, *Biased*, 129.

176   Kahneman notes, "In a famous study, spouses were asked, 'How large was your personal contribution to keeping the place tidy, in percentages?' They also answered similar questions about 'taking out the garbage,' 'initiating social engagements,' etc. Would the self-estimated contributions add up to 100%, or more, or less? As expected, the self-assessed contributions added up to more than 100%. The explanation is a simple availability bias: both spouses remember their own individual efforts and contributions much more clearly than those of the other, and the difference in availability leads to a difference in judged frequency." Kahneman, *Thinking, Fast and Slow*, 131.

177   Ibid., 97. Kahneman further presses the point: "We pay more attention to the content of messages than to information about their reliability, and as a result end up with a view of the world around us that is simpler and more coherent than the data justify." Ibid., 118.

178   Ibid., 79.

179   Ibid., 81.

180 See Thomas W. Hazlett, "Making the Fairness Doctrine Great Again," *Reason* (March 2018): 34-39 (https://reason.com/2018/02/15/making-the-fairness-doctrine-g/) and "The Broadcasting Fairness Doctrine," *Congressional Digest* 66, no. 10 (October 1987): 227.

181 Cass R. Sunstein, *The Law of Group Polarization*, John M. Olin Program in Law and Economics Working Paper No. 91 (Chicago: University of Chicago Law School, 1999), 2. Sunstein notes, "When people find themselves in groups of like-minded types, they are especially likely to move to extremes." Ibid.

182 Minchul Kim, Xiaoxia Cao, and Maria Elizabeth Grabe, "Assessing News Bias in the Age of a Polarized Media Environment: How Pre-Existing Skepticism toward a Partisan News Outlet Affects Perceived News Bias" (conference paper presented at the ICA Interactive Paper/Poster Session II, Prague, January 2018), 3.

183 Ibid.

184 Ibid., 12

185 Cass R. Sunstein, *Going to Extremes: How Like Minds Unite and Divide* (London: Oxford University Press, 2009), 3.

186 Cleveland, *Disunity in Christ*, 50.

187 Ibid., 51.

188 Ibid., 51.

189 Kahneman, *Thinking, Fast and Slow*, 85.

190 Eric Schmitt, "A Botched Drone Strike in Kabul Started with the Wrong Car," *The New York Times*, September 21, 2021, accessed September 23, 2021, https://www.nytimes.com/2021/09/21/us/politics/drone-strike-kabul.html.

191 Ibid.

192 According to one source, "The Afghan car population has skyrocketed recently, going from 175.000 in the whole of the country in 2002 to 500.000 in Kabul alone in 2010. A rough estimate is that 90% of all these cars are various generations of Toyota Corolla." Matt Gasnier, "Afghanistan Full Year 2017: Toyota Corolla Still King of the Roads," Best Selling Cars Blog (blog), January 25, 2018, accessed June 22, 2022, https://bestsellingcarsblog.com/2018/01/afghanistan-full-year-2017-toyota-corolla-still-king-of-the-roads/.

193   Kahneman, *Thinking, Fast and Slow*, 103.

Chapter 9: Second Metaphor—The Scout and the Soldier Mindsets

194   Julia Galef, *The Scout Mindset: Why Some People See Things Clearly and Others Don't* (New York: Penguin Publishing Group, 2018), 11.

195   Ibid.

196   Ibid., 12.

197   Ibid.

198   Ibid., 27.

199   Ibid., 20.

200   Ibid.

201   It is worth noting that the soldier/scout paradigm may prove helpful when applied to the reparations question, whether African American citizens should be compensated for unjust legal barriers that prevented them from accruing wealth. The issue received new attention after the March 2021, Evanston, IL City Council decision to grant reparations payments. (See Rachel Treisman, "In Likely First, Chicago Suburb of Evanston Approves Reparations for Black Residents," NPR, Code Switch, March 23, 2021, accessed April 2, 2021, https://www.npr.org/2021/03/23/980277688/in-likely-first-chicago-suburb-of-evanston-approves-reparations-for-black-reside.)

The city of Seattle, like many cities throughout the United States, had a red-lining policy in place until 1977 which effectively thwarted African Americans from moving outside of the Central District. The red-lining not only dictated the areas in which they could hold property, but it also depressed the value of the properties they did hold. African American landholders and business owners were also subjected to prejudicial lending policies, paying more interest than their White counterparts for an equivalent loan or being denied consideration for loans altogether. Home ownership and business ownership are recognized as the primary instrument through which the middle class accrues wealth.

The discriminatory practices of the past present the question "Does a just response to those wrongs compel reparative action in the present?" The answer one gives to the question may be significantly impacted by the mindset one adopts, whether scout or soldier. Haidt suggests that this question relates to the fairness foundation in ethics and that liberals and conservatives tend to interpret fairness differently. A liberal places more emphasis on fairness as proportionality; a conservative sees fairness from the perspective of freedom to choose (Haidt, *The Righteous Mind*, 192-216).

For historical artifacts relating to the Seattle history of redlining, see "Redlining and Disinvestment in Central Seattle: How the Banks Are Destroying Our Neighborhoods" (report, Central Seattle Community Council Federation, July 1975), accessed March 30, 2021, http://archives.seattle.gov/digital-collections/index.php/Detail/objects/243972.

For a discussion of the broader issue, see Darrick Hamilton and William Darity, "Can 'Baby Bonds' Eliminate the Racial Wealth Gap in Putative Post-Racial America?" *The Review of Black Political Economy* 37, no. 3-4 (January 1, 2010): 207-216. See also, Kriston McIntosh Shambaugh, Emily Moss, Ryan Nunn, and Jay Shambaugh, "Examining the Black-White Wealth Gap," Brookings Institute, February 27, 2020, accessed July 26, 2021, https://www.brookings.edu/blog/up-front/2020/02/27/examining-the-black-white-wealth-gap/.

202   Galef, *The Scout Mindset*, 32.

203   Ibid., 34.

204   CSPAN [@cspan]. "Bill Barr: 'There Was an Avalanche of All These Allegations of Fraud That Built up over a Number of Days and It Was like Trying to Play Whack-a-Mole … All the Early Claims That I Understood Were Completely Bogus and Silly and Usually Based on Complete Misinformation,'" Twitter, June 13, 2022, accessed July 12, 2022, https://twitter.com/cspan/status/1536376490304192513.

205   Domenico Montanaro, "'Just Say It Was Corrupt' and 3 Other Takeaways from Thursday's Jan. 6 Hearing," NPR, June 23, 2022, sec. Politics, accessed July 12, 2022, https://www.npr.org/2022/06/23/1106701188/just-say-it-was-corrupt-and-3-other-takeaways-from-thursdays-jan-6-hearing.

206   Kahneman names this tendency the "conjunction fallacy." Kahneman, *Thinking, Fast and Slow,* 159.

207   Galef, *The Scout Mindset*, 167.

208   *Ted Lasso*, Season 1, Episode 8, "The Diamond Dogs," directed by Declan Lowney, aired September 18, 2020, on Apple TV, https://www.youtube.com/watch?v=i_FofLSherM.

209   Galef, *The Scout Mindset*, 50.

210   Ibid., 51-57.

211   Ibid., 57.

212   Doris Kearns Goodwin, *Team of Rivals: The Political Genius of Abraham Lincoln* (New York: Simon & Schuster, 2006).

Chapter 10: Third Metaphor—The Rider and the Elephant

213   Morals may be defined as "the various principles regarding right and wrong, viewed individually or as comprising a whole, that constitute a standard for conduct and are seen as governing the way humans are to live." Stanley J. Grenz and Jay T. Smith, *Pocket Dictionary of Ethics: Over 300 Terms and Ideas Clearly and Concisely Defined* (Downers Grove, IL: InterVarsity Press, 2003), 77.

214   Jonathan Haidt, *The Righteous Mind* (New York: Vintage Books, 2012), 54.

215   Ibid., 53.

216   Ibid., xxi.

217   Ibid., 54.

218   Patricia S. Churchland, *Braintrust: What Neuroscience Tells Us about Morality* (Princeton, NJ: Princeton University Press, 2011), 12.

219   Richard Shweder, Haidt's mentor at the University of Chicago, demonstrated that one's ethical framework is significantly influenced by the social/cultural context in which one lives. Shweder developed a three-fold theory of morality, each layer emphasizing a different perspective on human nature informed by culture. The concept was first introduced in R. A. Shweder, "In Defense of Moral Realism: Reply to Gabennesch," *Child Development* 61 (1990): 2060-67. "The ethic of autonomy is based on the idea that people are, first and foremost, autonomous individuals with wants, needs and preferences." (Haidt, *The Righteous Mind*, 116). This ethic is dominant in utilitarian philosophy represented by John Stuart Mill and is the preferred ethic of individualistic societies like the United States. As Haidt notes, "The ethic of community is based on the idea that people are, first and foremost, members of larger entities such as families, teams, armies, companies, tribes and nations" (Ibid.). The most important factor in such cultures is that each individual fulfills their assigned role. Haidt expounds, "The ethic of divinity is based on the idea that people are, first and foremost, temporary vessels within which a divine soul has been implanted" (Ibid., 117). Ethical decision making in this setting implies aligning one's attitude and actions with God's will.

Most of the world consists of cultures that emphasize the ethics of community and of divinity. Haidt notes that "people from cultures that are Western, educated, industrialized, rich, and democratic (forming the acronym WEIRD) … are statistical outliers; they are the least typical, least representative people you could study if you want to make generalizations about human nature" (Ibid., 112). People in the United States tend push personal autonomy to an extreme even beyond their European counterparts, and this fact can be noted in the shape of their ethical decisions. Their ethical framework aligns with John Stuart Mill and Immanuel Kant, whose moral systems were "individualistic, rule-based, and universalist. That's the morality you need to govern a society of autonomous individuals" (Ibid.).

220　　Haidt, *The Righteous Mind*, 221.

221　　Ibid., 366.

222　　Ibid., 57.

223　　Martin Luther King, "Letter from Birmingham Jail," *The Atlantic Monthly*, August 1963, repr. February 2018, accessed October 1, 2021, https://www.theatlantic.com/magazine/archive/2018/02/letter-from-a-birmingham-jail/552461/.

Chapter 11: Factor #1 That Provokes Disunity: Ingroups and Outgroups

224　　Eberhardt, *Biased*, 13.

225　　Ibid., 14.

226　　Ibid., 33.

227　　Cleveland, *Disunity in Christ*, 47.

228　　*Oxford English Dictionary*, s.v. "bias," accessed September 27, 2021, https://www.oed.com/view/Entry/18564.

229　　Eberhardt, *Biased*, 31.

230　　Cleveland, *Disunity in Christ*, 82.

231　　Ibid., 84-85.

232　　Ibid., 88.

233   Malcolm Gladwell, *Talking to Strangers: What We Should Know about the People We Don't Know* (New York: Little, Brown and Company, 2019), 50.

234   From the poem by Mary T. Lathrap, "Judge Softly" (1895), AAA Native Arts Gallery, accessed October 1, 2021, https://www.aaanativearts.com/walk-mile-in-his-moccasins.

Chapter 12: Factor #2 That Provokes Disunity: Deficiency in the Social Capital of Trust

235   Ross Gittins, "Trust Makes the World Go Around, Honestly," *Sydney Morning Herald*, July 20, 2011, accessed October 15, 2021, https://www.smh.com.au/politics/federal/trust-makes-the-world-go-around-honestly-20110719-1hn4y.html.

236   See Francis Fukuyama, *Trust: The Social Virtues and the Creation of Prosperity* (New York: The Free Press, 1995). Fukuyama was one of the early voices arguing that trust serves as social capital and contributes significantly to economic flourishing.

237   David Brooks, "America Is Having a Moral Convulsion," *The Atlantic*, last modified October 5, 2020, accessed September 25, 2021, https://www.theatlantic.com/ideas/archive/2020/10/collapsing-levels-trust-are-devastating-america/616581/.

238   Sam Crosby, *The Trust Deficit* (Melbourne, AU: Melbourne University Press Digital, 2016), 26.

239   Liebermann contends that oxytocin works primarily to counteract the natural mammalian tendency to avoid the stranger. He calls it the "nurse neuropeptide," describing the selfless activity of nurses in caring for their patients with whom they have no special relationship nor enhanced level of trust. Liebermann, *Social*, 93.

240   Gladwell, *Talking to Strangers*, 72.

241   Ibid., 74.

242   "Public Trust in Government: 1958-2021," Pew Research Center, U.S. Politics & Policy, May 17, 2021, accessed September 26, 2021, https://www.pewresearch.org/politics/2021/05/17/public-trust-in-government-1958-2021/.

243   Ibid.

244   Brooks, "America Is Having a Moral Convulsion."

245   Ibid.

Chapter 13: Factor #3 That Provokes Disunity: Believing That Which Suits Us

246   See Lisa Lerer, "How Republican Vaccine Opposition Got to This Point," *The New York Times*, July 17, 2021, accessed September 28, 2021, https://www.nytimes.com/2021/07/17/us/politics/coronavirus-vaccines-republicans.html. See also Mark Jurkowitz and Amy Mitchell, "Americans Who Relied Most on Trump for COVID-19 News among Least Likely to Be Vaccinated," Pew Research Center, accessed September 28, 2021, https://www.pewresearch.org/fact-tank/2021/09/23/americans-who-relied-most-on-trump-for-covid-19-news-among-least-likely-to-be-vaccinated/.

247   It is beyond the scope of this project to address the differences in distrust between liberal and conservative leaning citizens. However, the distrust of public authority figures exhibited by Republicans has been significantly exacerbated by former President Trump's persistent attacks on authoritative spokespersons who disagree with him, especially in his accusations of "fake news." Kyle Conway observes, "In the time leading up to and immediately following the 2016 U.S. election, Americans were ripe for the idea of fake news. They didn't trust journalists. More than half thought that the news media were biased, regardless of their political affiliation. More than three-quarters of Republicans didn't trust the media, conservative Republicans being the least likely of all to trust them." Former President Trump did not invent the term *fake news*, but he shaped its meaning by using it in a consistent barrage against his critics. Kyle Conway, *The Art of Communication in a Polarized World* (Maxwell AFB, AL: AU Press, 2020), 99

248   Robert Farley, "Trump's Bogus Voter Fraud Claims," FactCheck.Org, October 19, 2016, accessed July 28, 2022, https://www.factcheck.org/2016/10/trumps-bogus-voter-fraud-claims/.

249   Ibid.

250   "Background on Trump's 'Voter Fraud' Commission | Brennan Center for Justice," accessed July 28, 2022, https://www.brennancenter.org/our-work/analysis-opinion/background-trumps-voter-fraud-commission.

251   For example, during the 2016 campaign, he correctly cited a Pew report that an estimated 1.8 million dead people remained on voter registration rolls but went on to assert that those people voted, an assertion that the article did not make. In fact, it stated that the instance of dead people's names being actually used in voting was exceptionally rare. Ibid.

252   Gladwell, *Talking to Strangers*, 78.

253   Kahneman, *Thinking, Fast and Slow*, 62.

254   Ibid.

255   A study released in July 2022 ought to serve as a definitive demonstration to conservative citizens that Trump's continued insistence that the election was rigged wholly lacks evidential support. See Senator John Danforth et al., "Lost, Not Stolen: The Conservative Case that Trump Lost and Biden Won the 2020 Presidential Election," Lost Not Stolen, accessed September 13, 2022,

https://lostnotstolen.org//wp-content/uploads/2022/07/Lost-Not-Stolen-The-Conservative-Case-that-Trump-Lost-and-Biden-Won-the-2020-Presidential-Election-July-2022.pdf. The authors consist of conservative lawyers, former judges and former Republican senators. The preface specifically states: "Every member of this informal group has worked in Republican politics, been appointed to office by Republicans, or is otherwise associated with the Party. None have shifted loyalties to the Democratic Party, and none bear any ill will toward Trump and especially not toward his sincere supporters" (Ibid., 3). They conclude that there is no evidence that voter fraud took place in the 2020 election sufficient to change the results in even a single precinct nationwide. They directly appeal to fellow Republicans who continue to support Trump's contention: "To have 30 percent of the country lack faith in election results based on unsubstantiated claims of a 'stolen' election is not sustainable in a democracy, and it discredits the political party making those charges" (Ibid., 7).

256   Georgia Secretary of State, "Historic First Statewide Audit of Paper Ballots Upholds Result of Presidential Race Elections," Office of Brad Raffensperger, accessed September 3, 2021,
https://sos.ga.gov/index.php/elections/historic_first_statewide_audit_of_paper_ballots_upholds_result_of_presidential_race.

257   Johnny Kauffman, "Inside the Battle for Fulton County's Votes," *Atlanta Magazine*, February 3, 2021, accessed October 18, 2021,
https://www.atlantamagazine.com/great-reads/inside-the-battle-for-fulton-countys-votes/.

See also Amara Walker, Chris Youd, and Ray Sanchez, "Family of Georgia's Secretary of State Was Still Getting Death Threats Months after Election, Report Says," CNN, accessed September 28, 2021, https://www.cnn.com/2021/06/11/politics/georgia-raffensperger-family-death-threats-election/index.html.

258   "Here's Every Word from the Fourth Jan. 6 Committee Hearing on its Investigation," NPR, June 21, 2022, accessed October 10, 2022, https://www.npr.org/2022/06/21/1105848096/jan-6-committee-hearing-transcript.

259   Ibid.

260   Philip Bump, "It's Not Clear that Donald Trump Understands the Relationship Between the President and the Military," Washington Post, September 8, 2016, accessed October 10, 2022, https://www.washingtonpost.com/news/the-fix/wp/2016/09/08/its-not-clear-that-donald-trump-understands-the-relationship-between-the-president-and-the-military/

261   Orin Kerr, "I know more about ISIS...," Twitter, accessed November 4, 2022, https://twitter.com/orinkerr/status/1252770601032433664?lang=en.

262   Christopher Krebs, "Opinion | Trump Fired Me for Saying This, But I'll Say It Again: The Election Wasn't Rigged," *Washington Post*, n.d., accessed July 19, 2022, https://www.washingtonpost.com/opinions/christopher-krebs-trump-election-wasnt-hacked/2020/12/01/88da94a0-340f-11eb-8d38-6aea1adb3839_story.html.

263   C. S. Lewis, *The Lion, the Witch and the Wardrobe* (New York: Collier Books, 1950), 45.

264   Sunstein, *The Law of Group Polarization*, 3-4.

265   Sunstein, *Going to Extremes*, 6.

266   Ibid., 7.

267   Ibid., 8.

268   Sunstein, *The Law of Group Polarization*, 6.

269   Sunstein recounts a fascinating study that compelled participants to defy their commonsense perception in order to conform to the group:

"A certain line was placed on a large white card. The task of the subjects was to 'match' that line by choosing, as identical to it in length, one of three other lines, placed on a separate large white card. One of the lines on the second white card was in fact identical in length to the line to be matched to it; the other two were substantially different, with the differential varying from an inch and three quarters to three quarters of an inch. The subject in the experiments was one of eight people asked to engage in the matching. But unbeknownst to the subject, the other people apparently being tested were actually there as part of the experiments.

"Asch's experiments unfolded in the following way. In the first two rounds, everyone agreed about the right answer; this seemed to be an extremely dull experiment. But the third round introduced 'an unexpected disturbance.' Other group members made what was obviously, to the subject and to any reasonable person, a clear error; they matched the line at issue to one that was obviously longer or shorter. In these circumstances the subject had the choice of maintaining his independent judgment or instead yielding to the crowd.

"A large number of people ended up yielding. In ordinary circumstances subjects erred less than 1 percent of the time; but in rounds in which group pressure supported the incorrect answer, subjects erred 36.8% of the time. Indeed, in a series of twelve questions, no less than 70% of subjects went along with the group, and defied the evidence of their own senses, at least once" (Ibid.).

270   David French, *Divided We Fall: America's Secession Threat and How to Restore Our Nation* (New York: St. Mary's Press, 2020), 2.

271   Alexis de Tocquevielle, *Democracy in America*, vols. 1 & 2, trans. Henry Reeve (Durham, NC: Duke Classics, 2012), 845.

272   French, *Divided We Fall*, 23.

273   Peter Wehner, *The Death of Politics: How to Heal Our Frayed Republic after Trump* (New York: HarperOne, 2021), 11.

274   Wehner asserts, "The opposition to compromise can be explained by several factors, including hyperpolarization in our politics, which creates an atmosphere in which compromise is viewed as betrayal; the belief that our political opponents are determined to destroy America, meaning that compromise amounts to treason; and the emergence in politics of what is referred to as the 'permanent campaign,' meaning the next campaign begins as soon as the last campaign ends." Ibid., 155.

275   Timothy Dalrymple, "The Splintering of the Evangelical Soul," *Christianity Today*, accessed June 22, 2021, https://www.christianitytoday.com/ct/2021/april-web-only/splintering-of-evangelical-soul.html.

276   Michael Graham, "The Six Way Fracturing of Evangelicalism," *Mere Orthodoxy*, last modified June 7, 2021, accessed June 22, 2021, https://mereorthodoxy.com/six-way-fracturing-evangelicalism/.

277   Ryan P. Burge and Paul A. Djupe, "Religious Authority in a Democratic Society: Clergy and Citizen Evidence from a New Measure," *Politics and Religion* 14 (April 2021): 5.

278   Burge and Djupe note that some studies distinguish between an authoritarian and an "authority-minded" point of view. "Authority-mindedness is rooted in adherents' commitment to the proposition that there is such a thing as ultimate authority and that true fulfillment in life can be found only by living under it." Ibid., 5.

279   Ibid., 6.

280   Gregory A. Smith, "More White Americans Adopted Than Shed Evangelical Label during Trump Presidency, Especially His Supporters," Pew Research Center, September 15, 2021, accessed September 28, 2021, https://www.pewresearch.org/fact-tank/2021/09/15/more-white-americans-adopted-than-shed-evangelical-label-during-trump-presidency-especially-his-supporters/.

281   David French argues, "What seems to be happening at scale isn't so much the growth of white Evangelicalism as a religious movement, but rather the near-culmination of the decades-long transformation of white Evangelicalism from a mainly religious movement into a Republican political cause." David French, "Did Donald Trump Make the Church Great Again?" *The Dispatch*, September 19, 2021, accessed September 20, 2021, https://frenchpress.thedispatch.com/p/did-donald-trump-make-the-church.

Chapter 14: Pathways toward Genuine Connection

282   Bryan Garsten, *Saving Persuasion: A Defense of Rhetoric and Judgment* (Cambridge, MA: Harvard University Press, 2009), 211-12.

283   Haidt, *The Righteous Mind*, 57.

284   Garsten, *Saving Persuasion*, 211.

285   Decades ago, one of my seminary professors offered a fitting quote that I have never been able to trace down to its origin. But I have often requoted it: "We cannot change anyone through direct action—we can only change ourselves. Then when we change, the other person may change in reaction to us."

286   Donald N. Larson, "The Viable Missionary: Learner, Trader, Story Teller," *Perspectives On the World Christian Movement*, 3rd ed. (Pasadena, CA: William Carey Library, 1999), 443.

287   Ibid.

288   Dale Carnegie, *How to Win Friends and Influence People*, rev. ed. (New York: Pocket Books, 1981), 37.

289   Haidt, *The Righteous Mind*, 58.

290   Everett L. Worthington Jr., "Fine-Tuning the Relationship between Religion and Intellectual Humility," *Journal of Psychology and Theology* 46, no. 4 (2018): 306.

291   Ibid., 307.

292   Daniel Rodriguez, et al., "Religious Intellectual Humility, Attitude Change, and Closeness Following Religious Disagreement," *The Journal of Positive Psychology* 14, no. 2 (2019): 134.

293   Worthington, "Fine-tuning the Relationship," 308.

294   Ibid., 309.

295   Rodriguez observes that intellectual humility is an important component in effecting actual change: "In the present study, which explored the aftermath of an actual disagreement discussion, IH was linked to both attitude change and feelings of closeness and trust with the discussion partner. Specifically, discussions in which both partners exhibited high levels of IH resulted in the greatest degree of attitude change." Rodriguez, "Religious Intellectual Humility," 139.

296   Worthington, "Fine-tuning the Relationship," 309.

297   For attribution, see James O'Donnell's scholarly discussion post, "A Common Quotation from 'Augustine'," Georgetown University, https://faculty.georgetown.edu/jod/augustine/quote.html.

298   P. M. Forni, *Choosing Civility: The Twenty-Five Rules of Considerate Conduct* (New York: St. Martin's Publishing Group, 2010), loc. 45, Kindle.

299   Ibid., loc. 383.

300   "Vision Statement," The Civility Project, Duluth Superior Area Community Foundation, accessed September 30, 2021, http://www.dsaspeakyourpeace.org/about.html.

301   Rules of engagement for the Speak Your Peace organization:

1. Pay attention. Be aware and attend to the world and the people around you.

2. Listen. Focus on others to better understand their points of view.

3. Be inclusive. Welcome all groups of citizens working for the greater good of the community.

4. Don't gossip. And don't accept when others choose to do so.

5. Show respect. Honor other people and their opinions, especially in the midst of disagreement.

6. Be agreeable. Look for opportunities to agree; don't contradict just to do so.

7. Apologize. Be sincere and repair damaged relationships.

8. Give constructive criticism. When disagreeing, stick to the issues and don't make a personal attack.

9. Take responsibility. Don't shift responsibility and blame onto others; share disagreements publicly (Ibid.).

302   Wehner, *The Death of Politics*, 183.

303   Daniel C. Dennett, *Intuition Pumps and Other Tools for Thinking* (New York: W. W. Norton & Company, 2013), 33-34.

304   See Edward C. Polson and Kevin D. Dougherty, "Worshiping across the Color Line: The Influence of Congregational Composition on Whites' Friendship Networks and Racial Attitudes," *Sociology of Race and Ethnicity* 5, no. 1 (January 1, 2019): 100–114.

305   Martin Luther King, Jr., "Interview on 'Meet the Press'" (transcript), April 17, 1960,
http://okra.stanford.edu/transcription/document_images/ Vol05Scans/17Apr1960_InterviewonMeetthePress.pdf.

306   Kevin D. Dougherty, Mark Chaves, and Michael O. Emerson, "Racial Diversity in U.S. Congregations, 1998-2019," *Journal for the Scientific Study of Religion* 59, no. 4 (2020): 651–662.

307   Polson and Dougherty, "Worshiping across the Color Line," 110.

308   Gordon Allport, *The Nature of Prejudice* (New York: Addison-Wesley, 1954).

309   Polson and Dougherty, "Worshiping across the Color Line," 101.

310   Cleveland, *Disunity in Christ*, 97.

311   As observed in chapter 11, the other-race effect has a dramatic impact on how we register facial characteristics, but its impact is nearly imperceptible to the person making the judgment. That does not excuse the casual comment of the pastor's friend, but it helps explain it. Eberhardt observes: "Scientists see the other-race effect as a sign that our perceptive powers are shaped by what we see. That cringe-worthy expression "They all look alike" has long been considered the province of the bigot. But it is actually a function of biology and exposure. Our brains are better at processing faces that evoke a sense of familiarity." Eberhardt, *Biased: Uncovering the Hidden Prejudice That Shapes What We See, Think, and Do*, 14.

312   Cleveland, *Disunity in Christ,* 187. Additionally: "Research on colorblind policies in integrated schools shows that teachers in these schools tend not to notice when students self-segregate, tend not to notice justice issues such as racial differences in student suspension rates and fail to incorporate teaching materials that represent the diversity of the students." Ibid.

313   Cleveland notes the difficulty of this: "To embrace our identities in this new, common family, we must engage in the difficult process of lessening our grip on the identities that we have idolized and clung to for far too long. In many ways, this process will jar our souls, wreaking havoc on the satisfyingly homogenous existence in which we are rooted. At first, it will feel painfully unnatural because we have lived outside of our true identities for so long that the truth seems wrong." Ibid., 189-190.

314   Sarah Stewart Holland and Beth Silvers, *I Think You're Wrong (But I'm Listening): A Guide to Grace-Filled Political Conversations* (Nashville, TN: Thomas Nelson, 2019), vi.

315   Ibid., 2.

316   Ibid., 9.

317   Ibid., xiv.

318   Ibid.

319   "Performing One Another: Theater Tools Help These Students Accept Different Perspectives," PBS NewsHour, last modified April 6, 2021, accessed April 23, 2021, https://www.pbs.org/newshour/show/performing-one-another-theater-tools-help-these-students-accept-different-perspectives.

320   Ibid.

321   Miroslav Volf, *Exclusion and Embrace: A Theological Exploration of Identity, Otherness, and Reconciliation* (Nashville: Abingdon Press, 1996), 141.

322   Ibid., 142.

323   Ibid., 143.

324   Ibid.

325   Ibid.

326   Ibid.

327   Ibid., 144.

328   Ibid., 145.

Chapter 15: Concluding with Three Central Implications

329   Aleksandr Solzhenitsyn, *The Gulag Archipelago*, vol.1 (New York: Harper and Row, 1973), 163.

Glossary

330   Kahneman, *Thinking, Fast and Slow*, 86.

331   Aaron Chalmers, "The Influence of Cognitive Biases on Biblical Interpretation," *Bulletin for Biblical Research* 26, no. 4 (2016): 470.

332   Kahneman, *Thinking, Fast and Slow*, 97.

333   Chalmers, "The Influence of Cognitive Biases on Biblical Interpretation," 474.

334   *Merriam-Webster Dictionary*, s.v. "partisanship," accessed October 13, 2021, https://www.merriam-webster.com/dictionary/partisanship.

335   Jonathan Haidt, *The Righteous Mind* (New York: Vintage Books, 2012), 245.

336   Carl Bradford, "A Gospel-Centered Approach to the Issue of Racism: Race, Ethnicity, and the Gospel's Influence towards Racial Reconciliation," *Southwestern Journal of Theology* 63, no. 2 (2021): 106.

337   Stanley J. Grenz and Jay T. Smith, *Pocket Dictionary of Ethics: Over 300 Terms and Ideas Clearly and Concisely Defined* (Downers Grove, IL: InterVarsity Press, 2003), 101.

338   *Merriam-Webster Dictionary*, s.v. "tolerance," accessed October 11, 2011, http://www.merriam-webster.com/dictionary/tolerance.